I WAS ALWAYS A WEIRD KID, WITHIN WHAT IS CONSIDERED "NORMAL". WHEN I WAS EIGHT YEARS OLD, MY PARENTS GAVE ME THE INCREDIBLE NEVER-ENDING STORY BY MICHAEL ENDE, AND INSTEAD OF PLAYING SOCCER OR BASEBALL LIKE THE REST OF MY FRIENDS, I SPENT MY AFTERNOONS READING AND DRAWING. WHENEVER I LEFT THE HOUSE, IT WAS TO DRAG THE REST OF THE GROUP ON AN ADVENTURE TO THE NEARBY FOREST OR RIVER. I GREW UP AND THAT ADVENTUROUS SPIRIT GREW WITH ME, TO SUCH AN EXTENT THAT, WITHOUT STOPPING WRITING AND DRAWING, I DEDICATED MY PROFESSIONAL LIFE TO HELPING OTHERS, IN THE EMERGENCY CORPS OF MY COUNTRY. SOONER RATHER THAN LATER, MY BELOVED DAUGHTER ARRIVED, AND WITHOUT REALIZING IT, TIME BEGAN TO RUN VERY FAST, POSTPONING PROJECTS IN EXCHANGE FOR SEEING HER GROW AND SHARING MY ADVENTUROUS SPIRIT WITH HER. WELL, TODAY, ON THE VERGE OF MY FORTIETH BIRTHDAY, I HAVE FINALLY DECIDED TO PUBLISH SOMETHING, IT'S NOT MUCH, JUST SOME CHARACTERS AND THEIR SHEETS TO USE IN ROLE-PLAYING GAMES. EVEN WITHOUT BEING MUCH, IT IS PART OF SOMETHING BIGGER, BECAUSE THE PROJECT I HAVE IN MY HANDS WILL NOT DISAPPOINT THOSE WHO, LIKE ME, DID NOT PLAY SOCCER WHEN THEY WERE KIDS. I HOPE YOU ENJOY IT, AND TO GET IN TOUCH WITH ME, SEE MORE OF MY ART OR ANYTHING ELSE, FOLLOW ME ON INSTAGRAM, @RICKYCARTOONART , BECAUSE THERE I WILL BE UPLOADING CONTENT TO KEEP YOU UP TO DATE WITH MY PROJECTS. THANKS FOR GIVING ME THE OPPORTUNITY TO SURPRISE YOU!!!!

RICKY CARTOONART

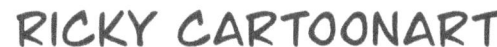

I0446872

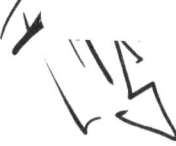

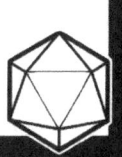

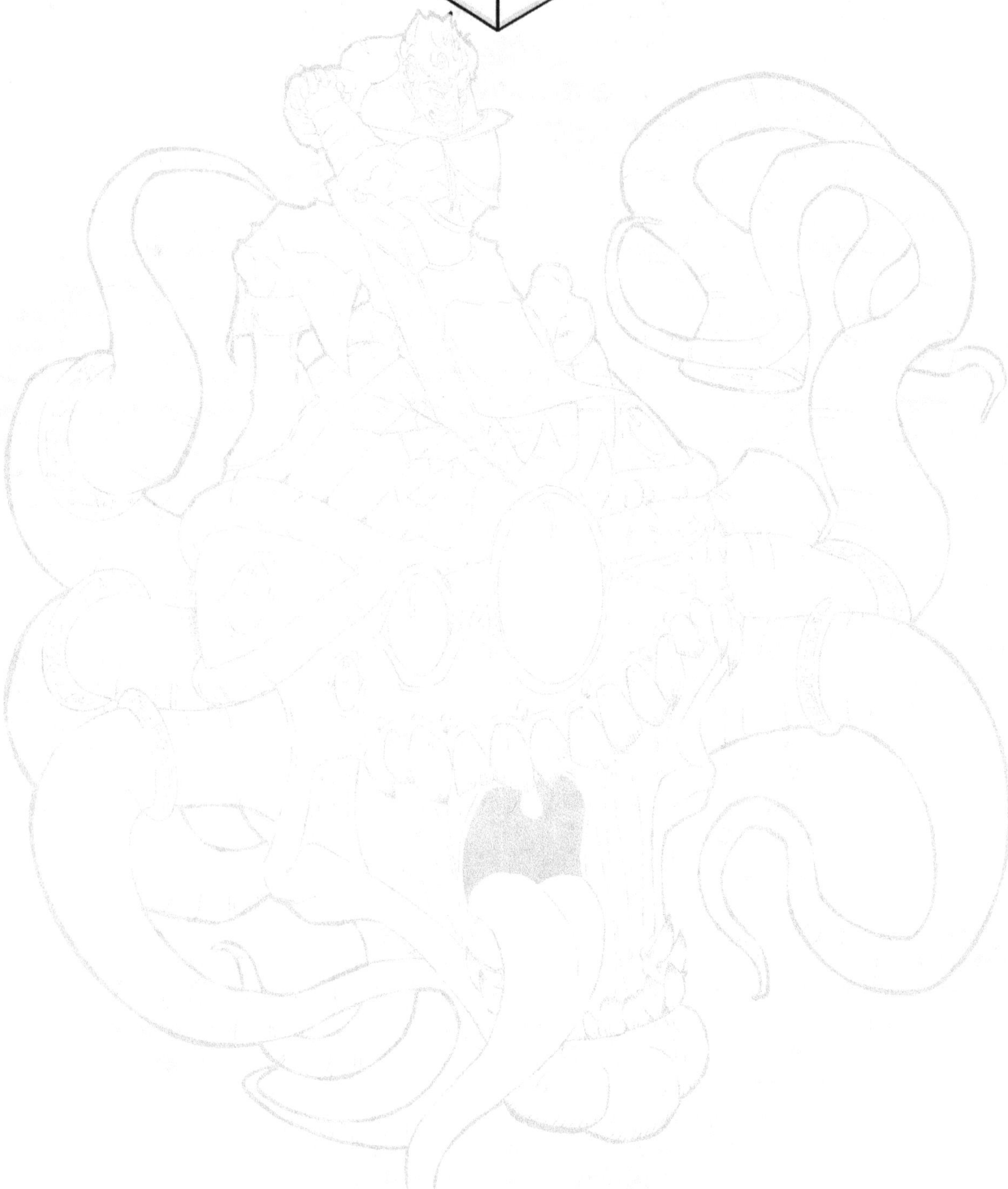

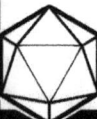

Adventure Logbook

RD20

RICKY CARTOONART

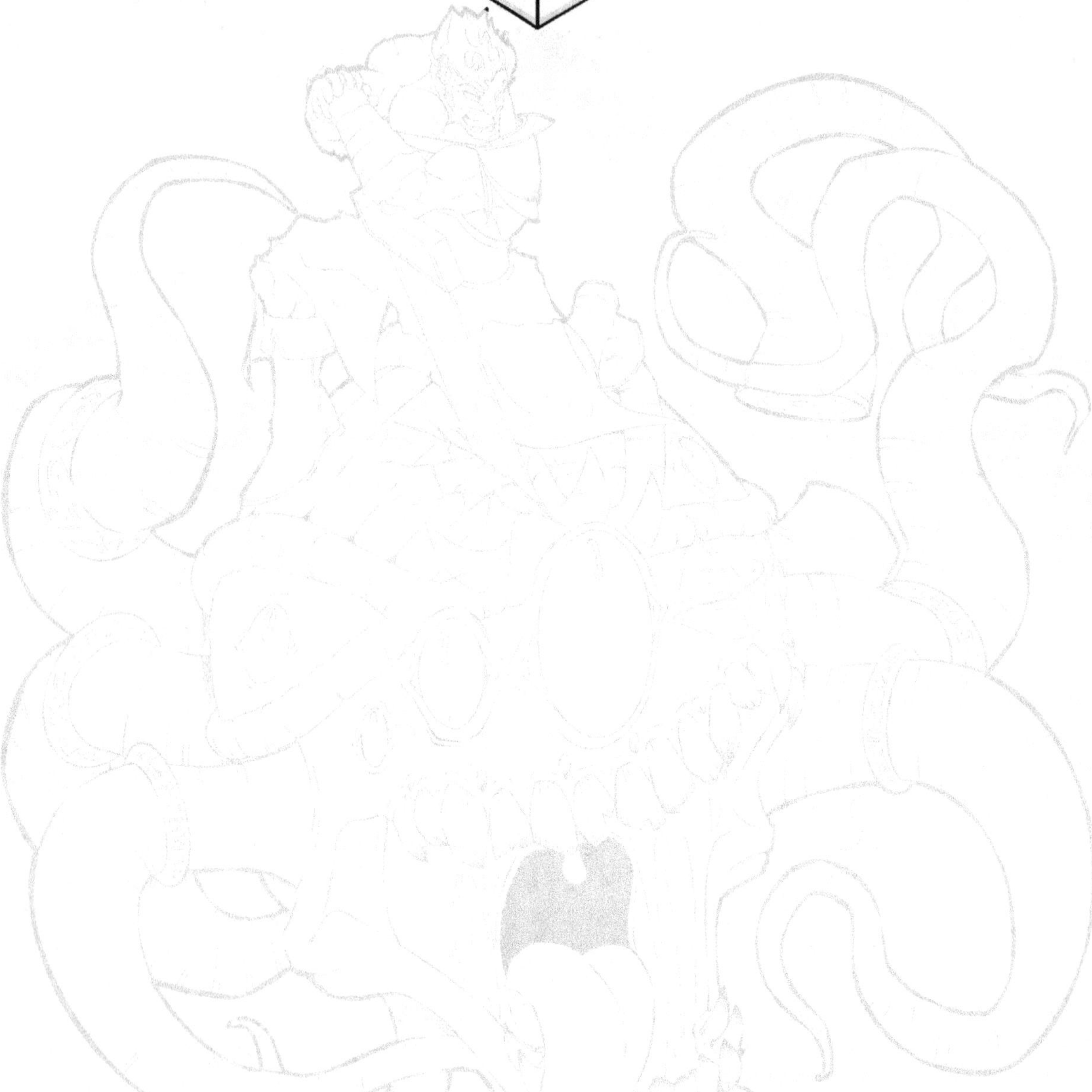

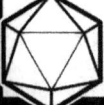

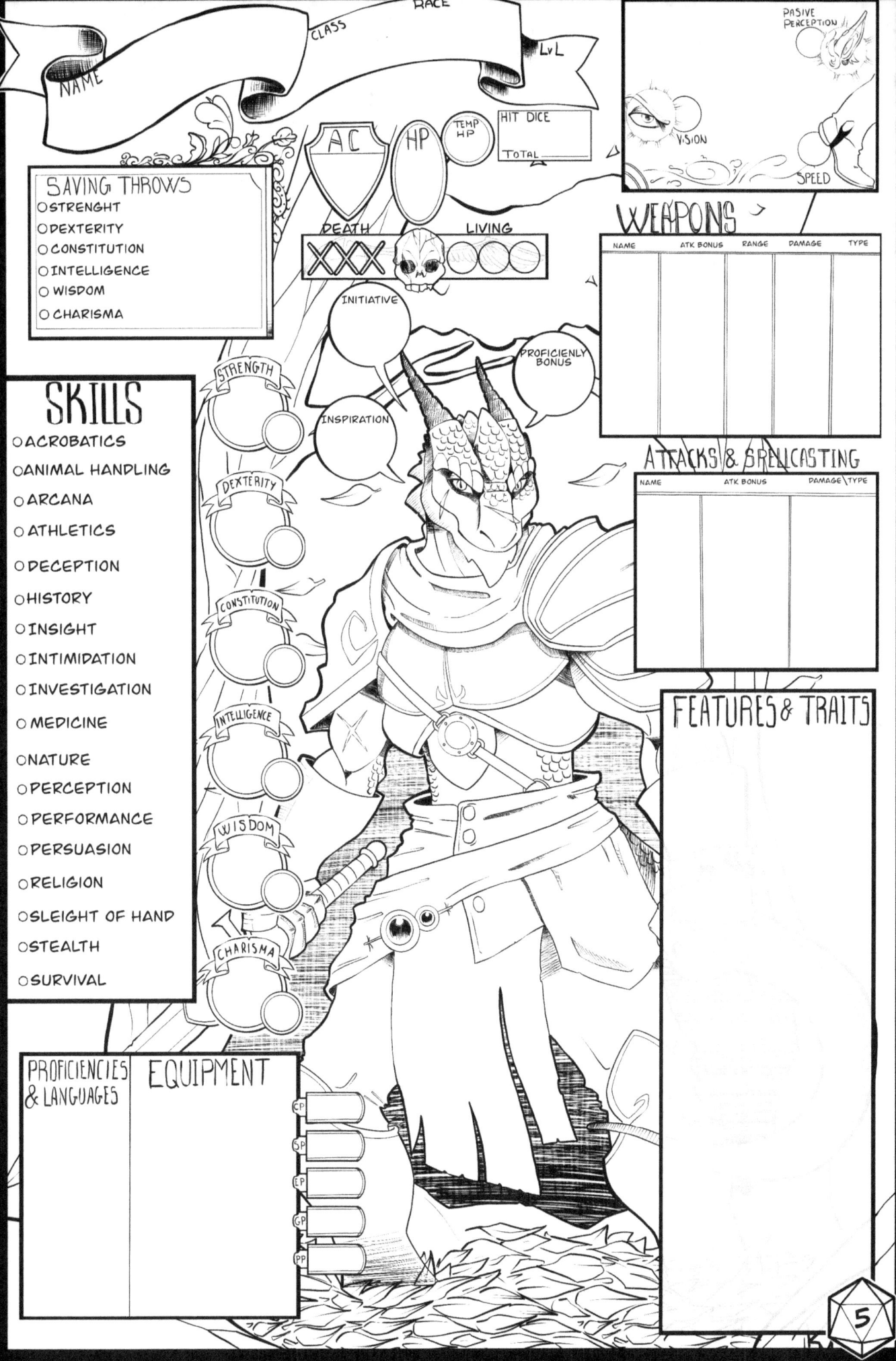

NAME

CLASS RACE LvL

AC HP TEMP HP HIT DICE TOTAL

PASIVE PERCEPTION

VISION

SPEED

DEATH LIVING

SAVING THROWS
- STRENGHT
- DEXTERITY
- CONSTITUTION
- INTELLIGENCE
- WISDOM
- CHARISMA

INITIATIVE

PROFICIENLY BONUS

INSPIRATION

WEAPONS

NAME	ATK BONUS	RANGE	DAMAGE	TYPE

ATTACKS & SPELLCASTING

NAME	ATK BONUS	DAMAGE\TYPE

SKILLS
- ACROBATICS
- ANIMAL HANDLING
- ARCANA
- ATHLETICS
- DECEPTION
- HISTORY
- INSIGHT
- INTIMIDATION
- INVESTIGATION
- MEDICINE
- NATURE
- PERCEPTION
- PERFORMANCE
- PERSUASION
- RELIGION
- SLEIGHT OF HAND
- STEALTH
- SURVIVAL

STRENGTH

DEXTERITY

CONSTITUTION

INTELLIGENCE

WISDOM

CHARISMA

FEATURES & TRAITS

PROFICIENCIES & LANGUAGES

EQUIPMENT

CP
SP
EP
GP
PP

5

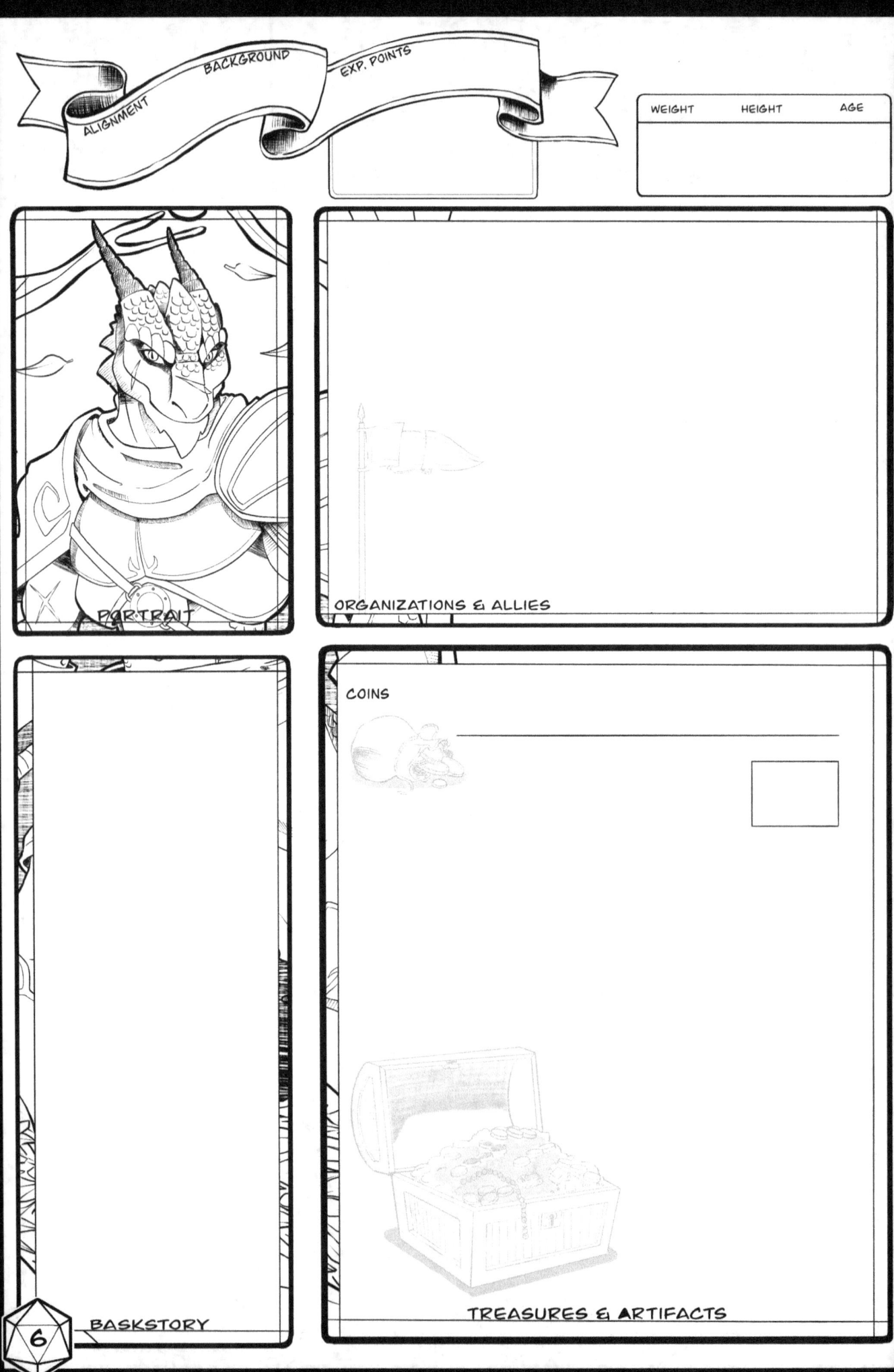

ALIGNMENT   BACKGROUND   EXP. POINTS

WEIGHT   HEIGHT   AGE

PORTRAIT

ORGANIZATIONS & ALLIES

COINS

BASKSTORY

TREASURES & ARTIFACTS

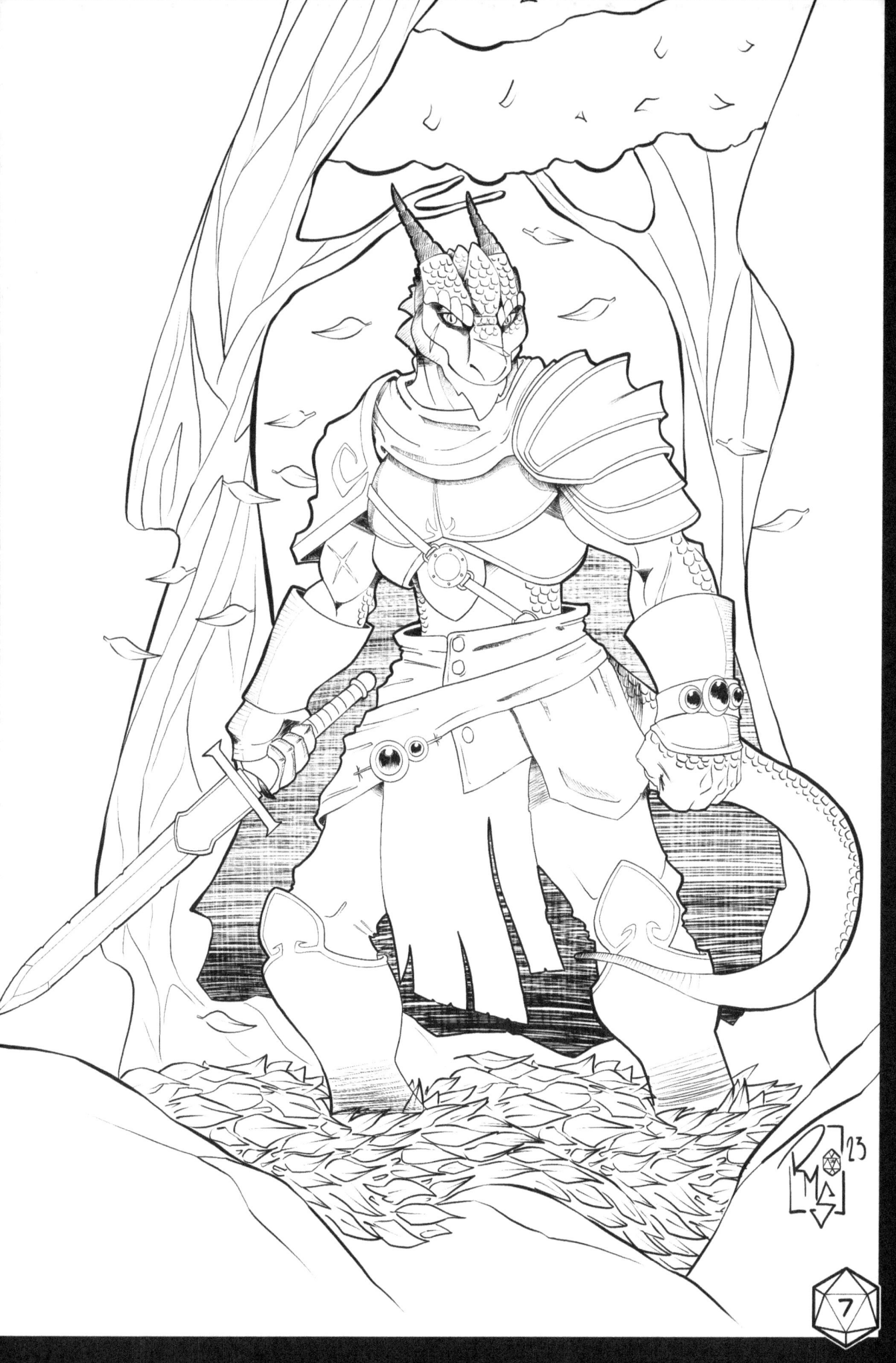

ON THIS PAGE, YOU CAN WRITE DOWN ANY RELEVANT MATTER OF THE STORY AND ADVENTURES THAT YOUR CHARACTER LIVES: THE CLUE ABOUT A TREASURE, THE MAP OF A DUNGEON, RUMORS ABOUT THE WHEREABOUTS OF A RELEVANT PERSON... IT'S YOUR ADVENTURE, MAKE IT EPIC!

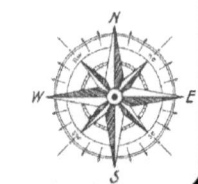

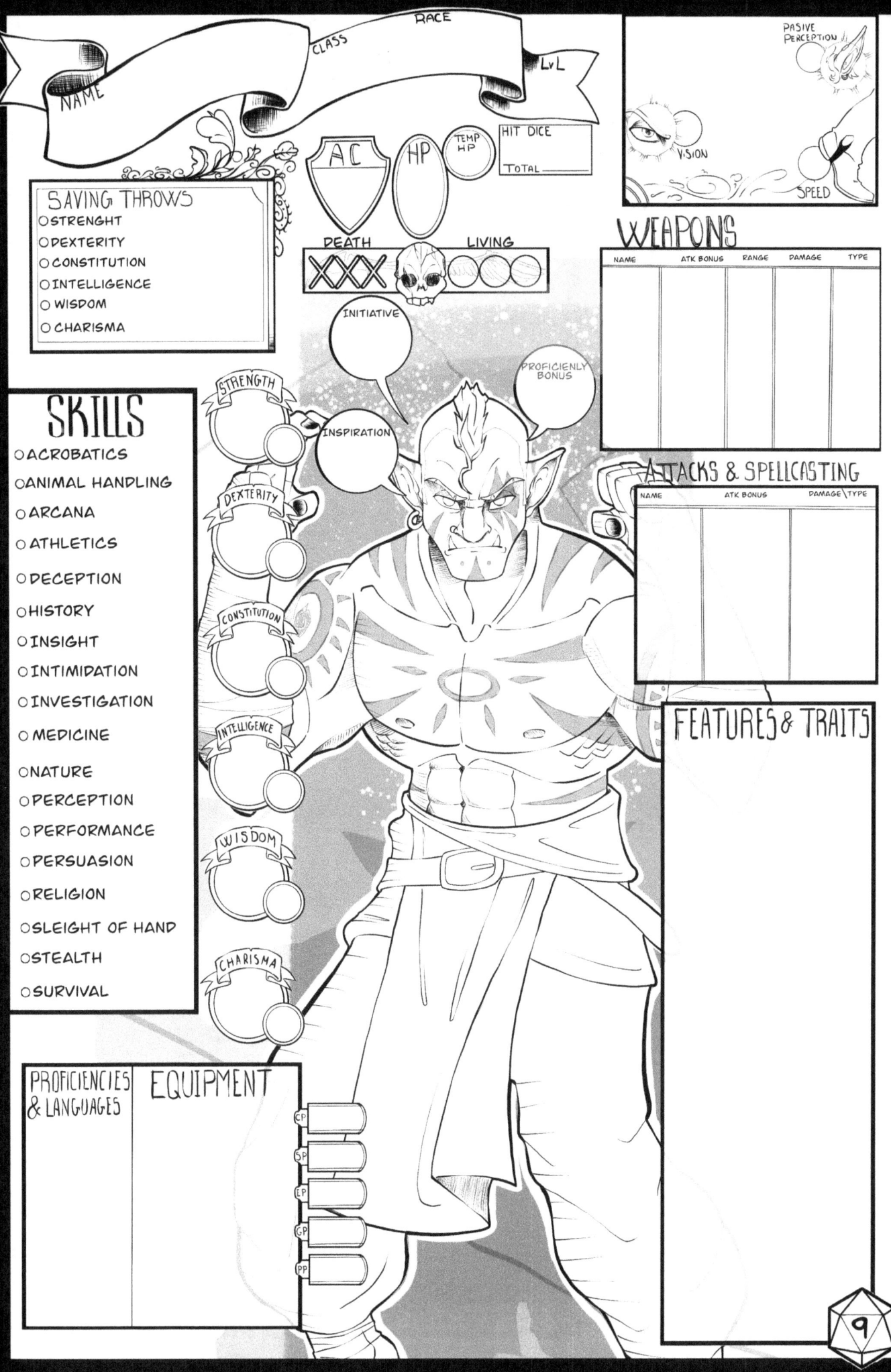

NAME

CLASS RACE LvL

PASIVE PERCEPTION

VISION SPEED

AC HP TEMP HP

HIT DICE
TOTAL _____

DEATH LIVING

XXX ○○○

INITIATIVE

PROFICIENLY BONUS

INSPIRATION

SAVING THROWS
○ STRENGHT
○ DEXTERITY
○ CONSTITUTION
○ INTELLIGENCE
○ WISDOM
○ CHARISMA

WEAPONS

NAME	ATK BONUS	RANGE	DAMAGE	TYPE

ATTACKS & SPELLCASTING

NAME	ATK BONUS	DAMAGE\TYPE

SKILLS
○ ACROBATICS
○ ANIMAL HANDLING
○ ARCANA
○ ATHLETICS
○ DECEPTION
○ HISTORY
○ INSIGHT
○ INTIMIDATION
○ INVESTIGATION
○ MEDICINE
○ NATURE
○ PERCEPTION
○ PERFORMANCE
○ PERSUASION
○ RELIGION
○ SLEIGHT OF HAND
○ STEALTH
○ SURVIVAL

STRENGTH

DEXTERITY

CONSTITUTION

INTELLIGENCE

WISDOM

CHARISMA

FEATURES & TRAITS

PROFICIENCIES & LANGUAGES

EQUIPMENT

CP
SP
EP
GP
PP

9

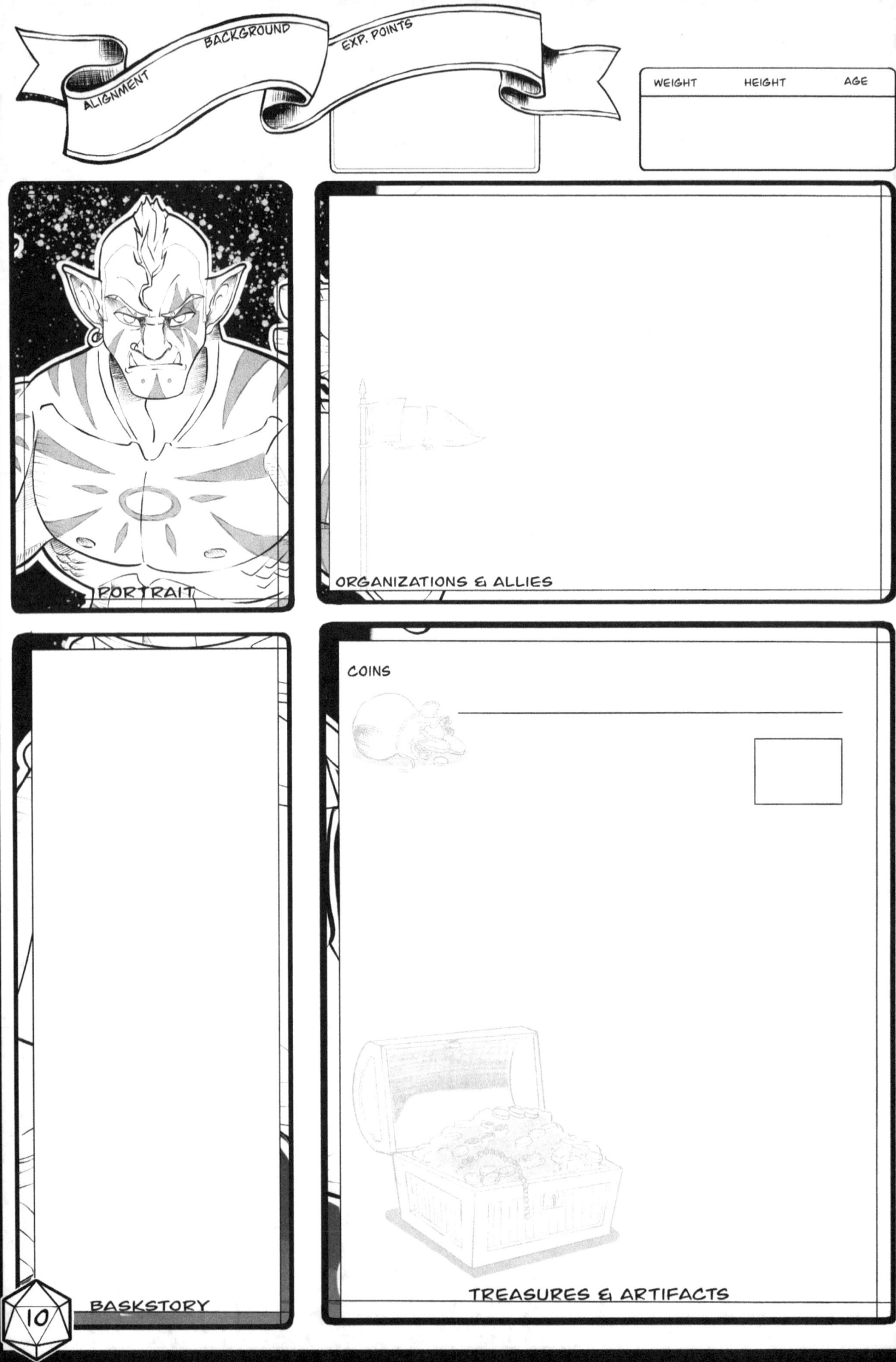

ALIGNMENT · BACKGROUND · EXP. POINTS

WEIGHT · HEIGHT · AGE

PORTRAIT

ORGANIZATIONS & ALLIES

COINS

BASKSTORY

TREASURES & ARTIFACTS

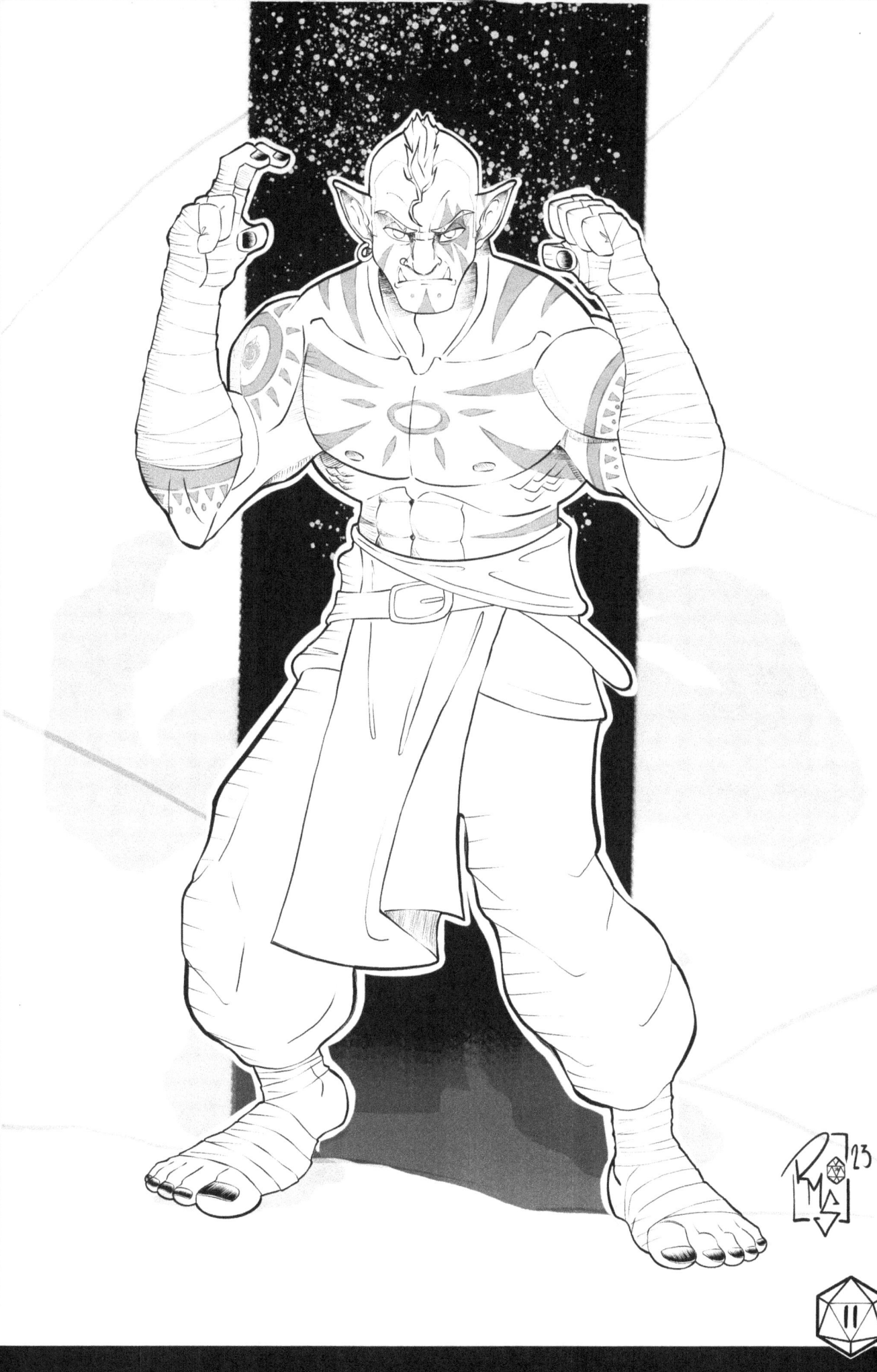

ON THIS PAGE, YOU CAN WRITE DOWN ANY RELEVANT MATTER OF THE STORY AND ADVENTURES THAT YOUR CHARACTER LIVES: THE CLUE ABOUT A TREASURE, THE MAP OF A DUNGEON, RUMORS ABOUT THE WHEREABOUTS OF A RELEVANT PERSON... IT'S YOUR ADVENTURE, MAKE IT EPIC!

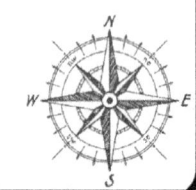

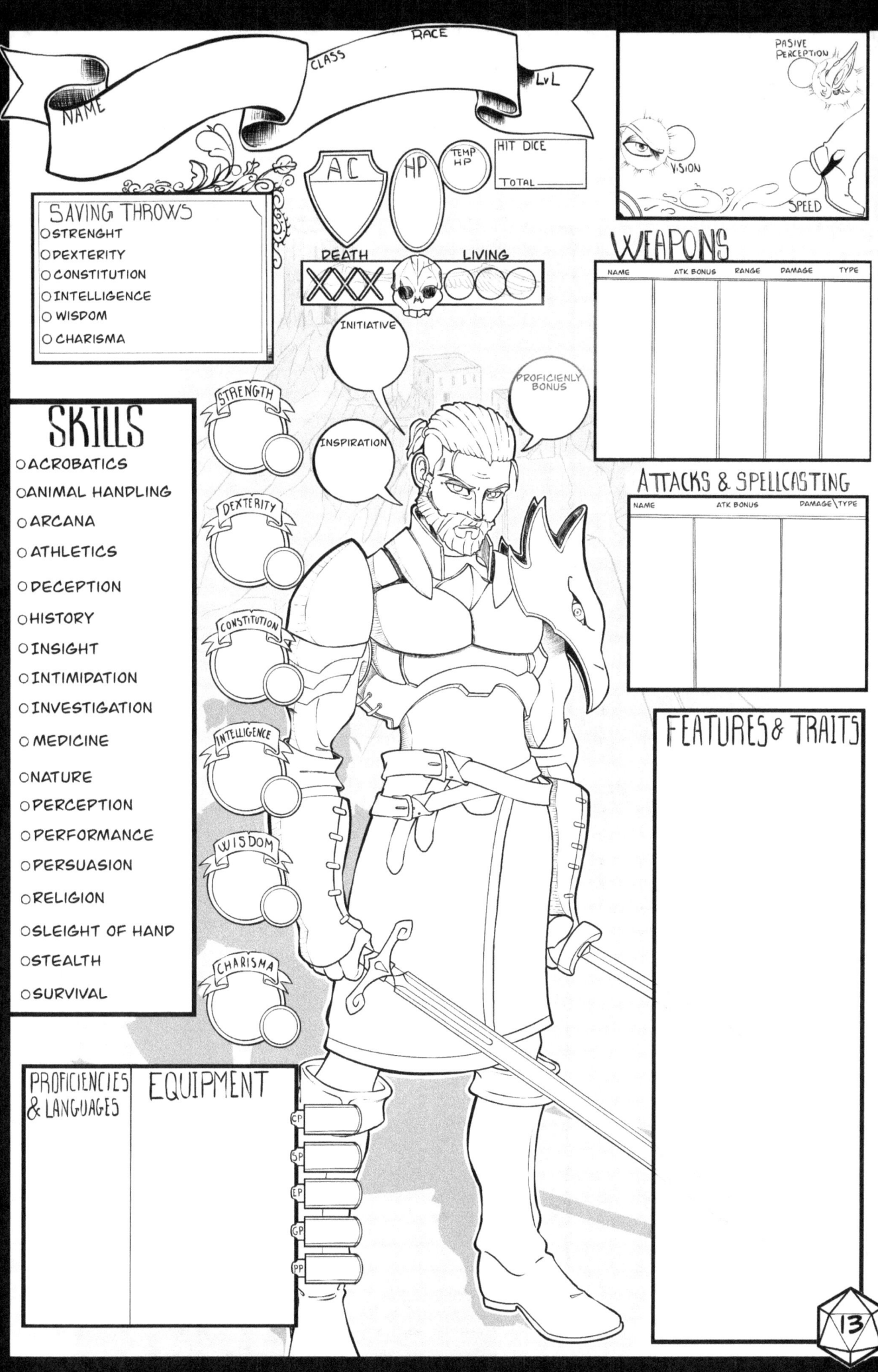

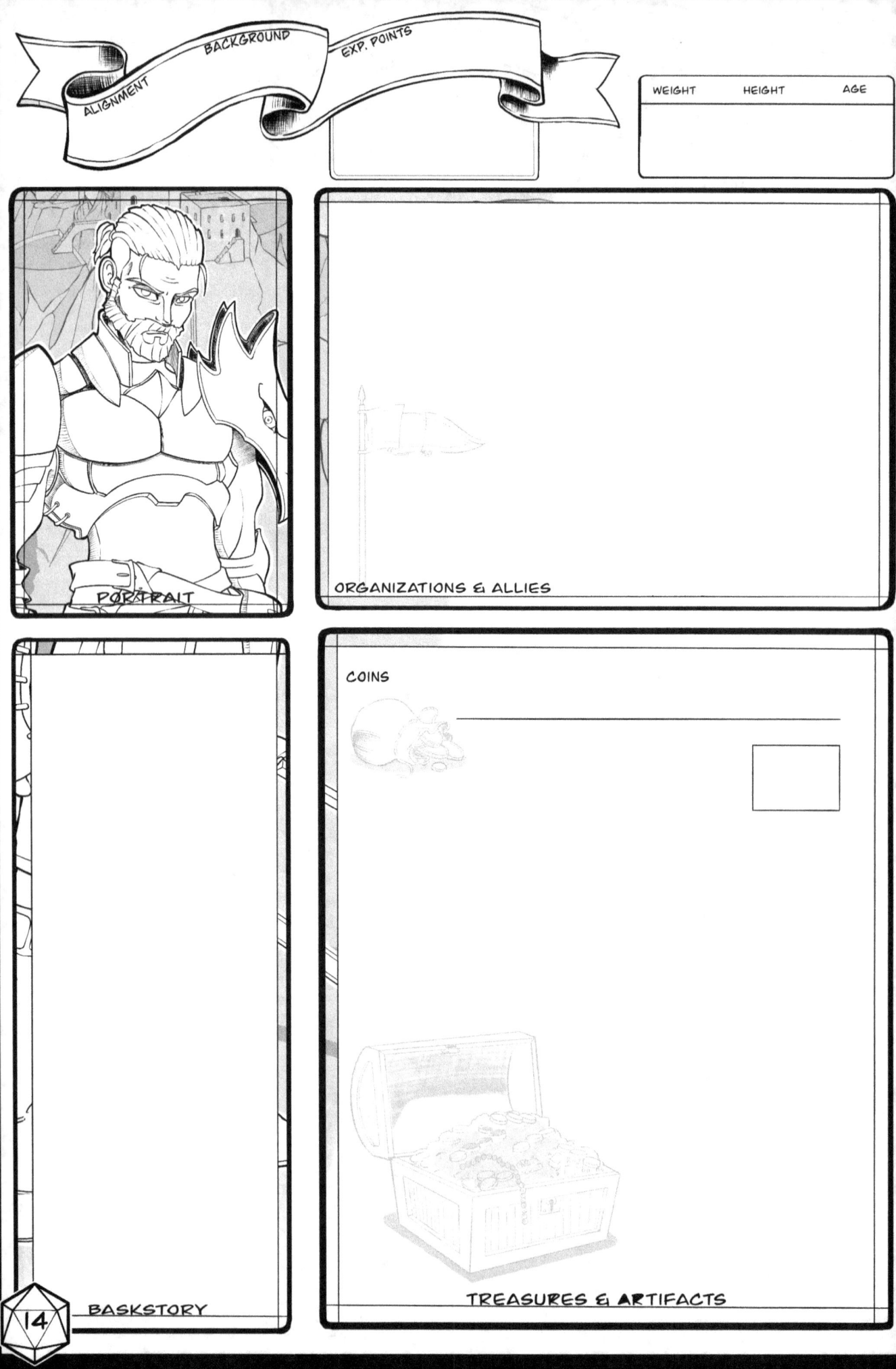

ALIGNMENT   BACKGROUND   EXP. POINTS

WEIGHT   HEIGHT   AGE

PORTRAIT

ORGANIZATIONS & ALLIES

COINS

BASKSTORY

TREASURES & ARTIFACTS

14

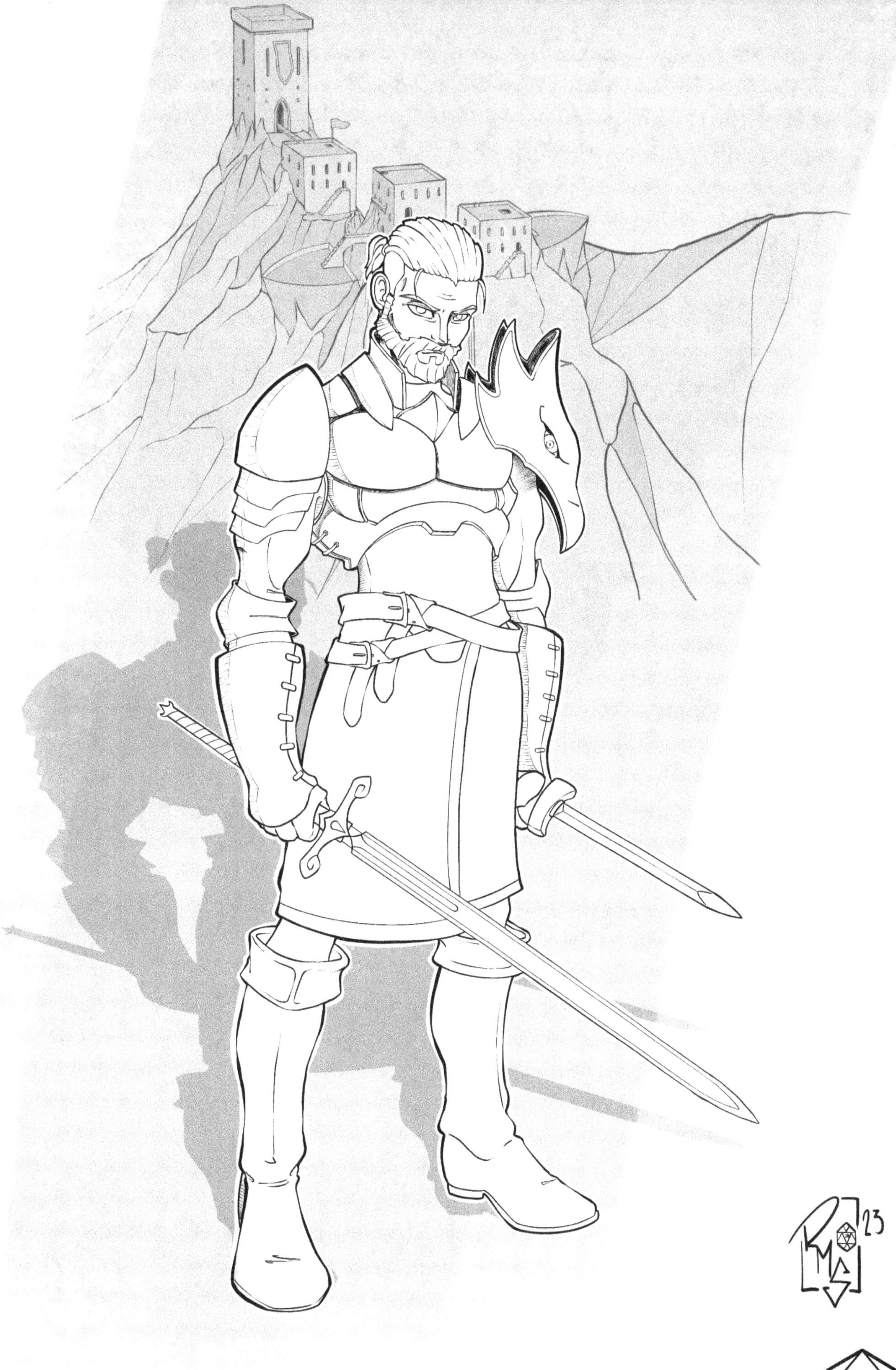

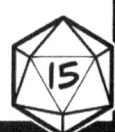

ON THIS PAGE, YOU CAN WRITE DOWN ANY RELEVANT MATTER OF THE STORY AND ADVENTURES THAT YOUR CHARACTER LIVES: THE CLUE ABOUT A TREASURE, THE MAP OF A DUNGEON, RUMORS ABOUT THE WHEREABOUTS OF A RELEVANT PERSON... IT'S YOUR ADVENTURE, MAKE IT EPIC!

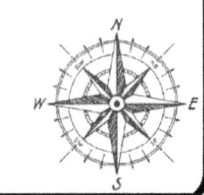

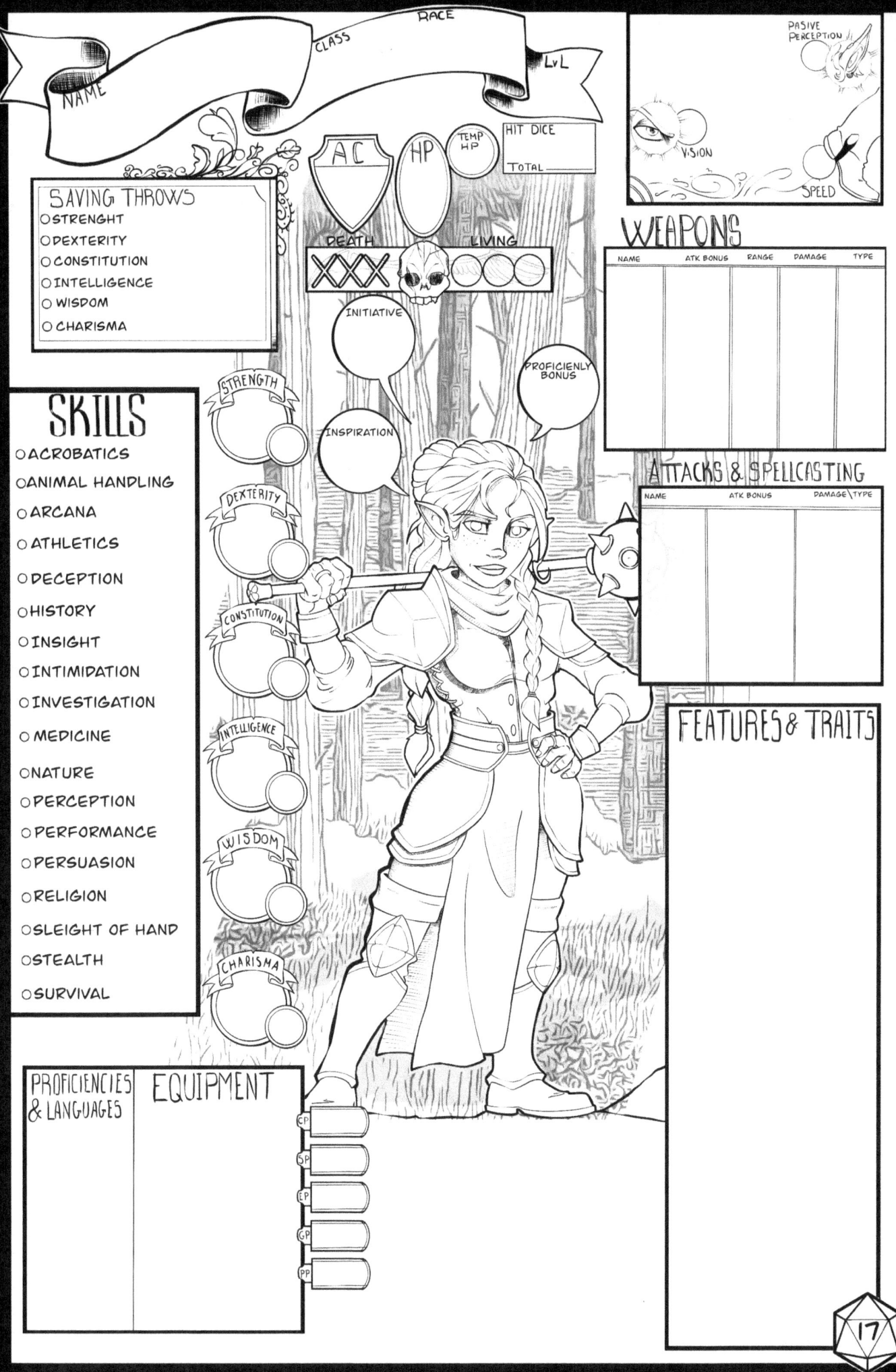

NAME

CLASS

RACE

LvL

AC HP TEMP HP

HIT DICE
TOTAL

PASIVE PERCEPTION

VISION

SPEED

SAVING THROWS
- STRENGHT
- DEXTERITY
- CONSTITUTION
- INTELLIGENCE
- WISDOM
- CHARISMA

DEATH LIVING

INITIATIVE

INSPIRATION

PROFICIENLY BONUS

SKILLS
- ACROBATICS
- ANIMAL HANDLING
- ARCANA
- ATHLETICS
- DECEPTION
- HISTORY
- INSIGHT
- INTIMIDATION
- INVESTIGATION
- MEDICINE
- NATURE
- PERCEPTION
- PERFORMANCE
- PERSUASION
- RELIGION
- SLEIGHT OF HAND
- STEALTH
- SURVIVAL

STRENGTH

DEXTERITY

CONSTITUTION

INTELLIGENCE

WISDOM

CHARISMA

WEAPONS

NAME	ATK BONUS	RANGE	DAMAGE	TYPE

ATTACKS & SPELLCASTING

NAME	ATK BONUS	DAMAGE\TYPE

FEATURES & TRAITS

PROFICIENCIES & LANGUAGES

EQUIPMENT

CP
SP
EP
GP
PP

17

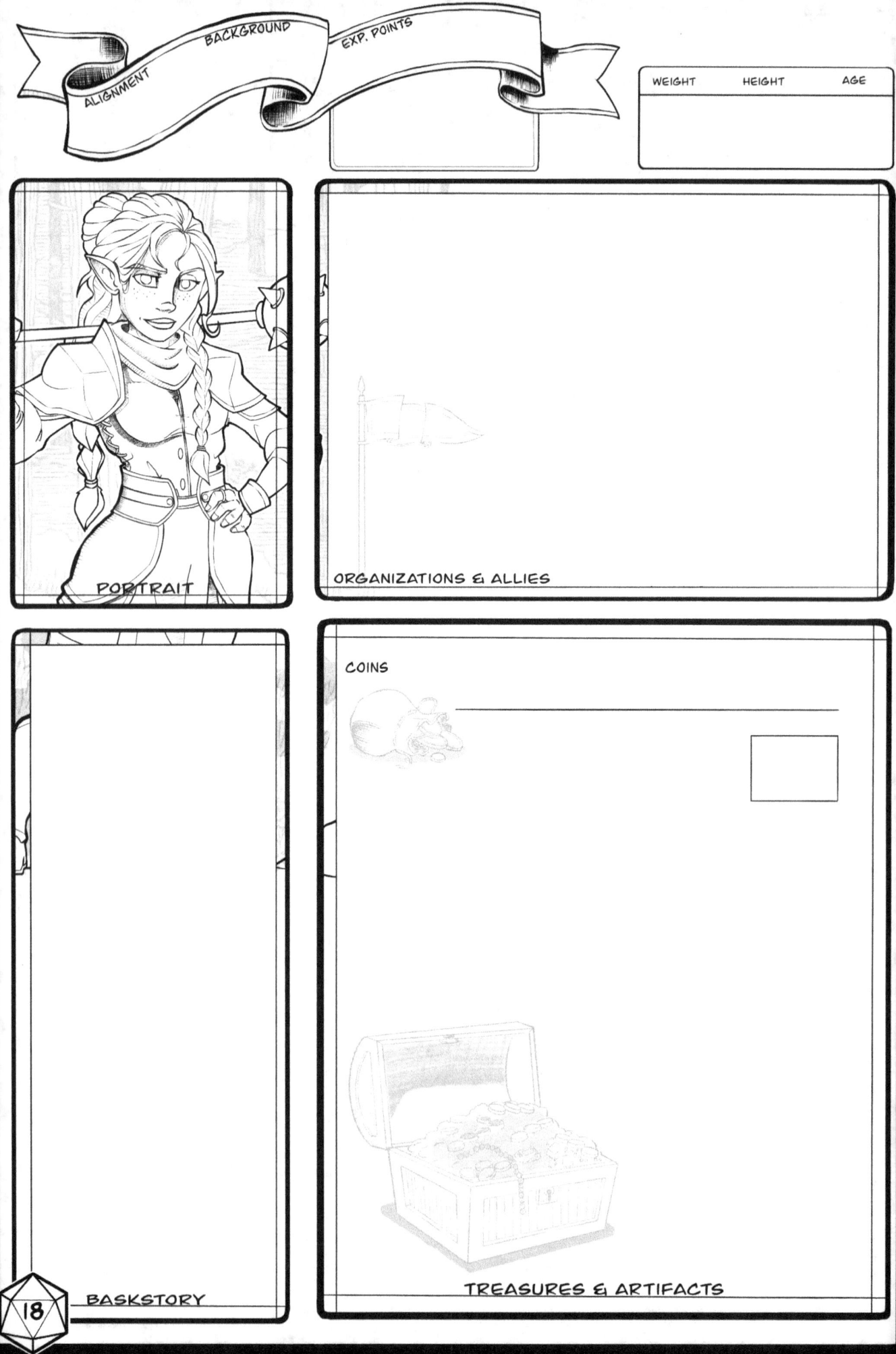

ALIGNMENT   BACKGROUND   EXP. POINTS

WEIGHT   HEIGHT   AGE

PORTRAIT

ORGANIZATIONS & ALLIES

COINS

BASKSTORY

TREASURES & ARTIFACTS

18

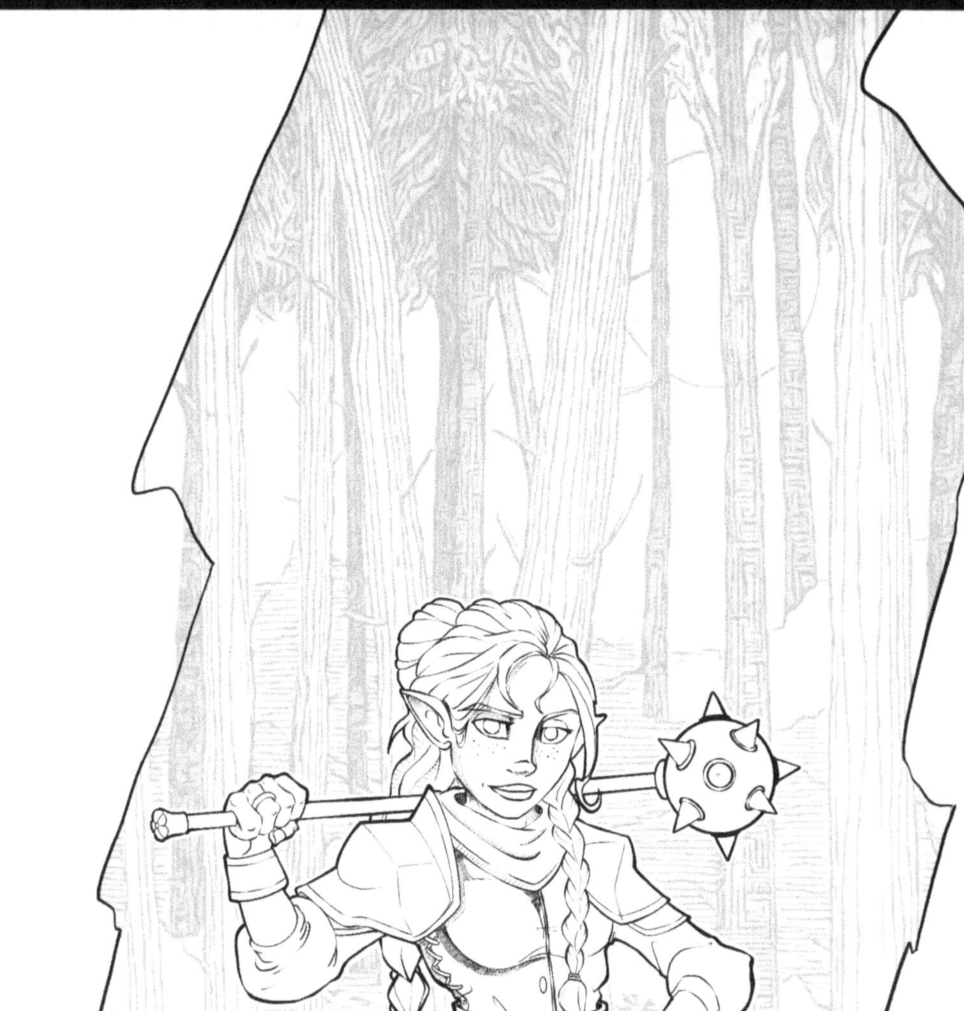

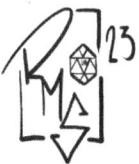

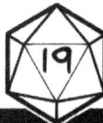

19

ON THIS PAGE, YOU CAN WRITE DOWN ANY RELEVANT MATTER OF THE STORY AND ADVENTURES THAT YOUR CHARACTER LIVES: THE CLUE ABOUT A TREASURE, THE MAP OF A DUNGEON, RUMORS ABOUT THE WHEREABOUTS OF A RELEVANT PERSON... IT'S YOUR ADVENTURE, MAKE IT EPIC!

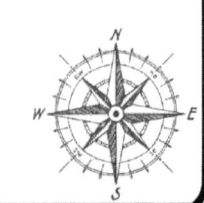

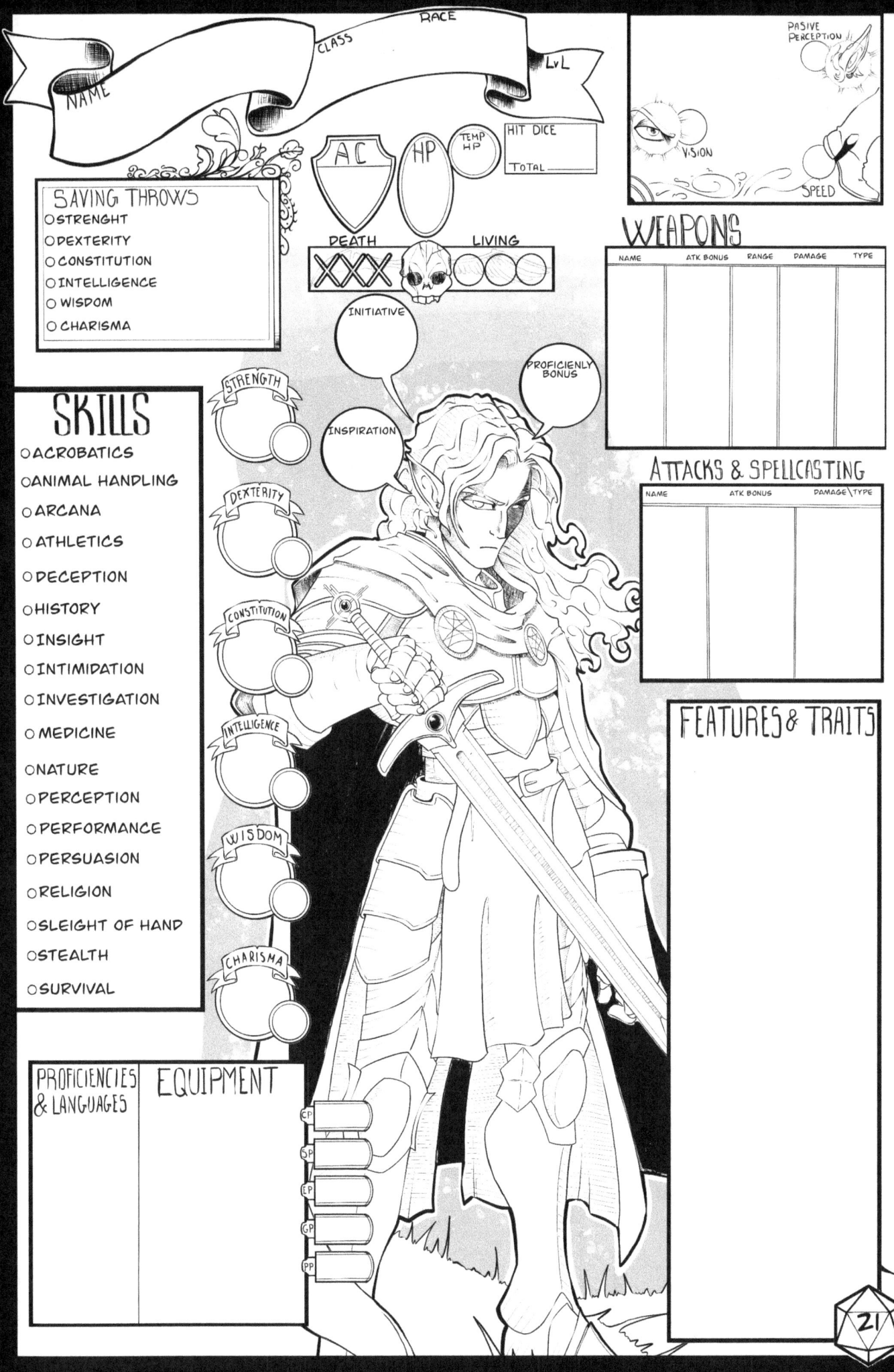

NAME

CLASS   RACE   LvL

PASIVE PERCEPTION

VISION

SPEED

AC   HP   TEMP HP

HIT DICE

TOTAL ___

DEATH   LIVING   ✕✕✕ ⚬⚬⚬

SAVING THROWS
○ STRENGHT
○ DEXTERITY
○ CONSTITUTION
○ INTELLIGENCE
○ WISDOM
○ CHARISMA

INITIATIVE

INSPIRATION

PROFICIENLY BONUS

WEAPONS

NAME	ATK BONUS	RANGE	DAMAGE	TYPE

SKILLS
○ ACROBATICS
○ ANIMAL HANDLING
○ ARCANA
○ ATHLETICS
○ DECEPTION
○ HISTORY
○ INSIGHT
○ INTIMIDATION
○ INVESTIGATION
○ MEDICINE
○ NATURE
○ PERCEPTION
○ PERFORMANCE
○ PERSUASION
○ RELIGION
○ SLEIGHT OF HAND
○ STEALTH
○ SURVIVAL

STRENGTH

DEXTERITY

CONSTITUTION

INTELLIGENCE

WISDOM

CHARISMA

ATTACKS & SPELLCASTING

NAME	ATK BONUS	DAMAGE\TYPE

FEATURES & TRAITS

PROFICIENCIES & LANGUAGES

EQUIPMENT

CP
SP
EP
GP
PP

21

ALIGNMENT   BACKGROUND   EXP. POINTS

WEIGHT   HEIGHT   AGE

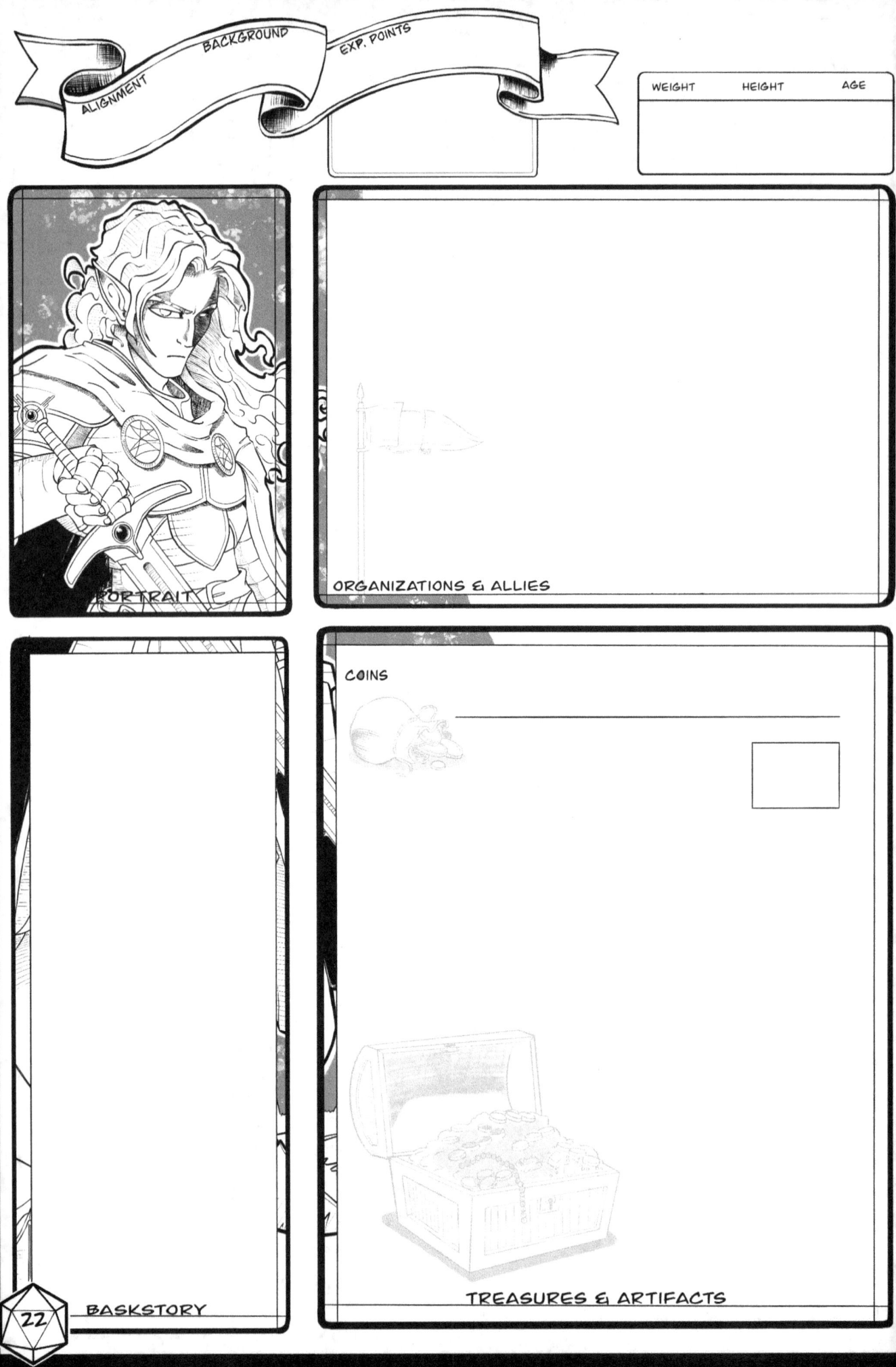

PORTRAIT

ORGANIZATIONS & ALLIES

COINS

BASKSTORY

TREASURES & ARTIFACTS

22

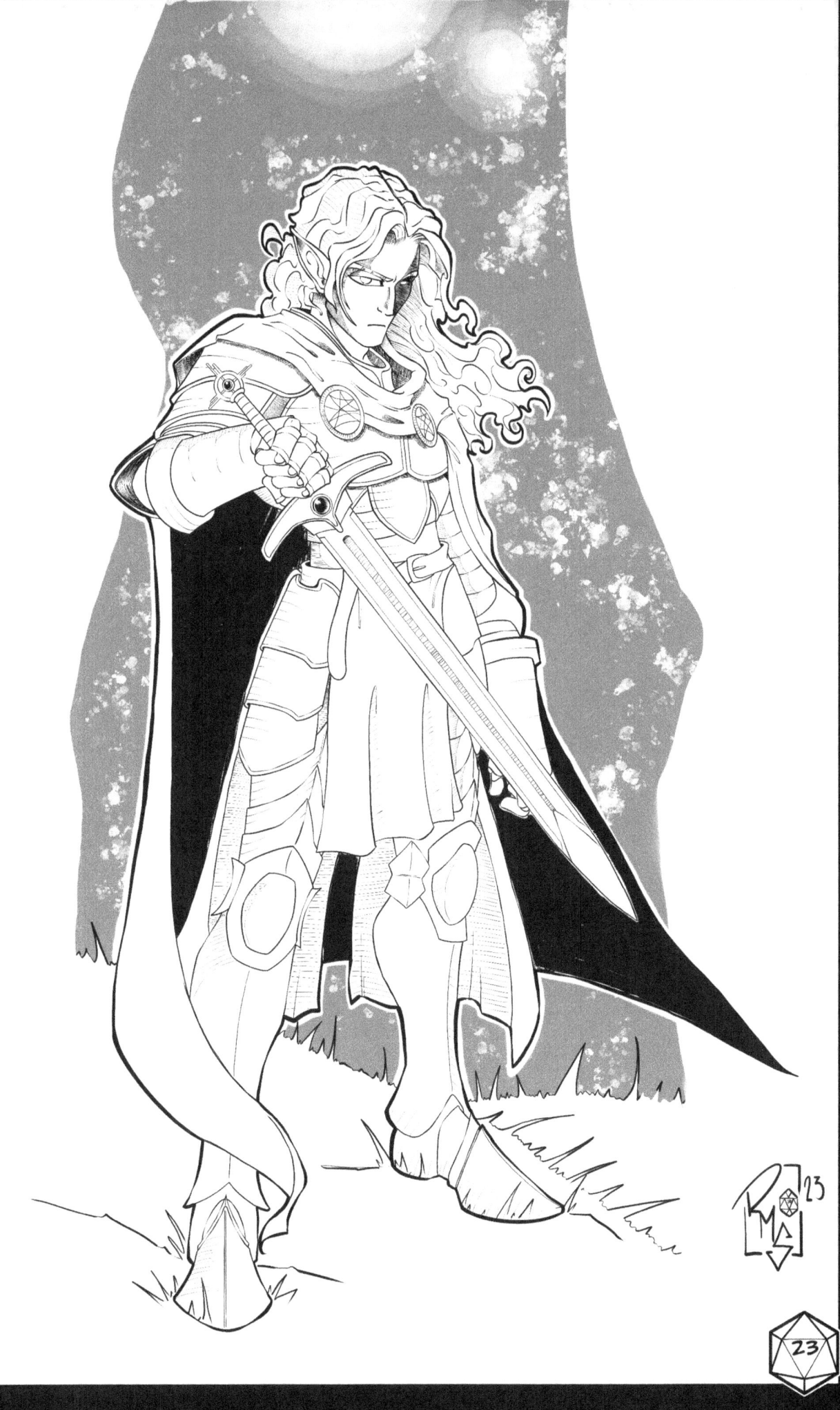

ON THIS PAGE, YOU CAN WRITE DOWN ANY RELEVANT MATTER OF THE STORY AND ADVENTURES THAT YOUR CHARACTER LIVES: THE CLUE ABOUT A TREASURE, THE MAP OF A DUNGEON, RUMORS ABOUT THE WHEREABOUTS OF A RELEVANT PERSON... IT'S YOUR ADVENTURE, MAKE IT EPIC!

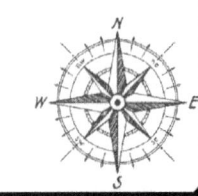

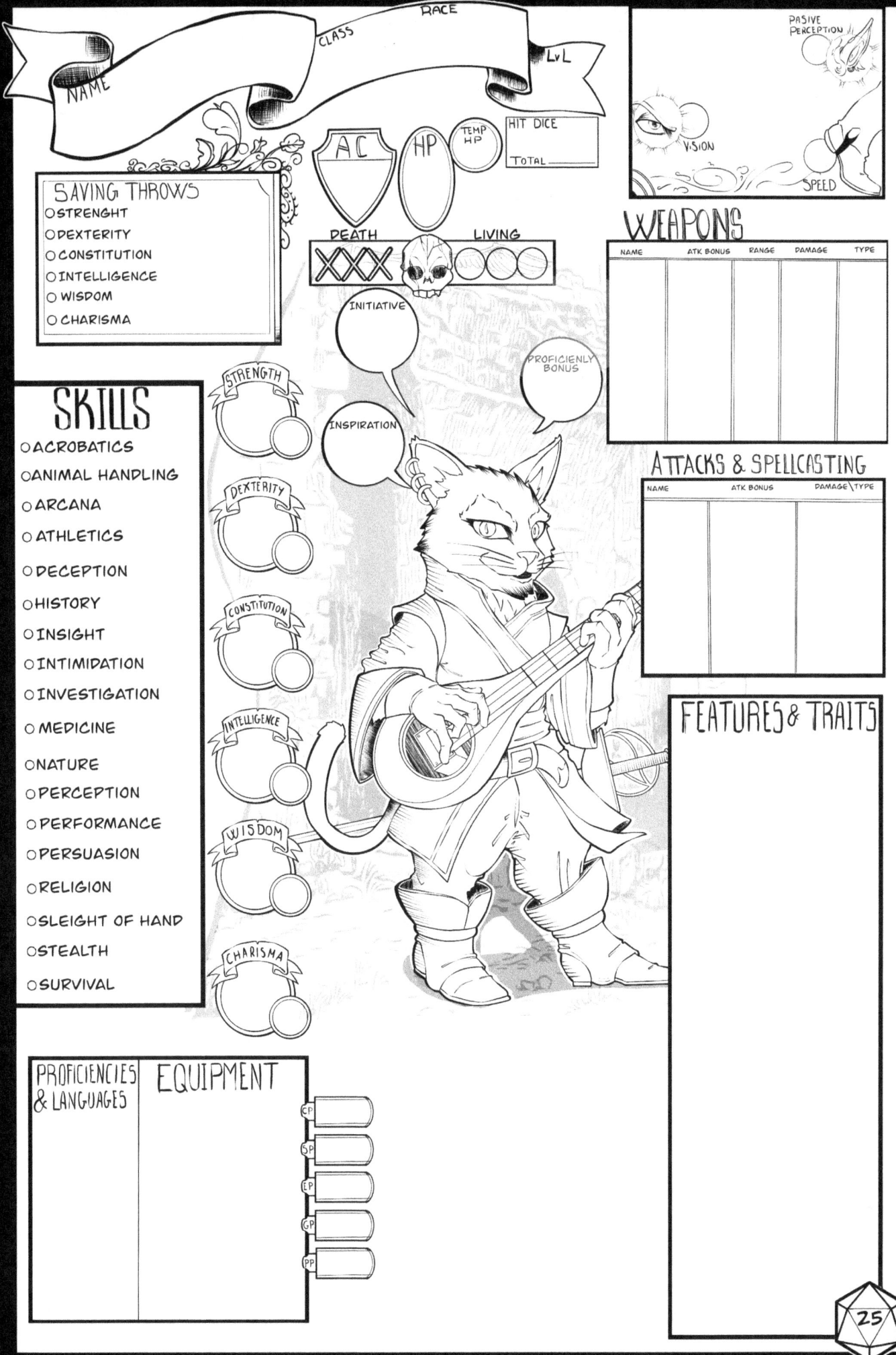

NAME

CLASS · RACE · LvL

PASIVE PERCEPTION

VISION · SPEED

AC · HP · TEMP HP

HIT DICE

TOTAL ____

SAVING THROWS
- ○ STRENGHT
- ○ DEXTERITY
- ○ CONSTITUTION
- ○ INTELLIGENCE
- ○ WISDOM
- ○ CHARISMA

DEATH · LIVING

INITIATIVE

INSPIRATION

PROFICIENLY BONUS

WEAPONS

NAME	ATK BONUS	RANGE	DAMAGE	TYPE

ATTACKS & SPELLCASTING

NAME	ATK BONUS	DAMAGE\TYPE

SKILLS
- ○ ACROBATICS
- ○ ANIMAL HANDLING
- ○ ARCANA
- ○ ATHLETICS
- ○ DECEPTION
- ○ HISTORY
- ○ INSIGHT
- ○ INTIMIDATION
- ○ INVESTIGATION
- ○ MEDICINE
- ○ NATURE
- ○ PERCEPTION
- ○ PERFORMANCE
- ○ PERSUASION
- ○ RELIGION
- ○ SLEIGHT OF HAND
- ○ STEALTH
- ○ SURVIVAL

STRENGTH

DEXTERITY

CONSTITUTION

INTELLIGENCE

WISDOM

CHARISMA

FEATURES & TRAITS

PROFICIENCIES & LANGUAGES

EQUIPMENT

CP · SP · EP · GP · PP

25

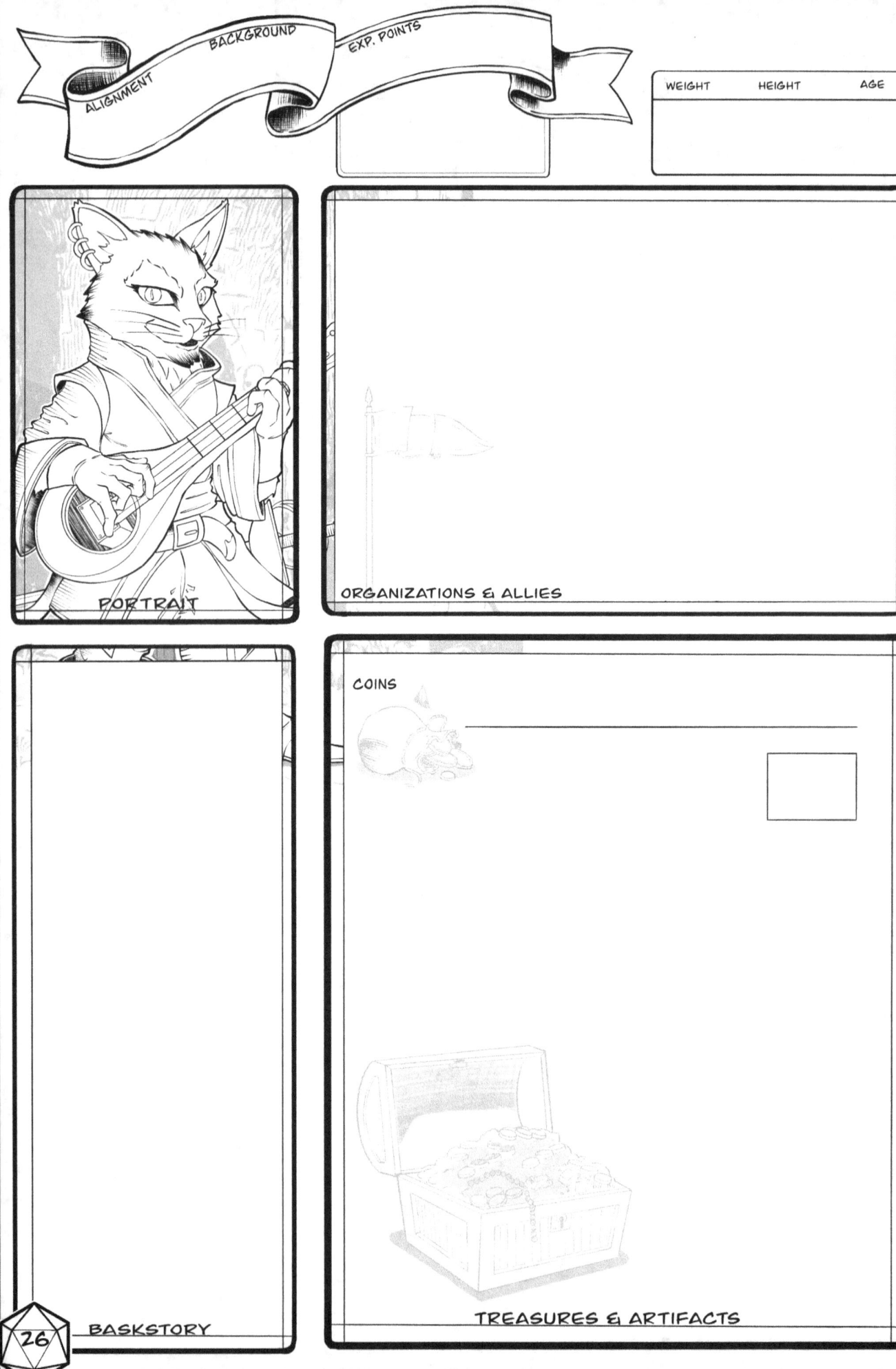

ALIGNMENT BACKGROUND EXP. POINTS

WEIGHT   HEIGHT   AGE

PORTRAIT

ORGANIZATIONS & ALLIES

COINS

BASKSTORY

TREASURES & ARTIFACTS

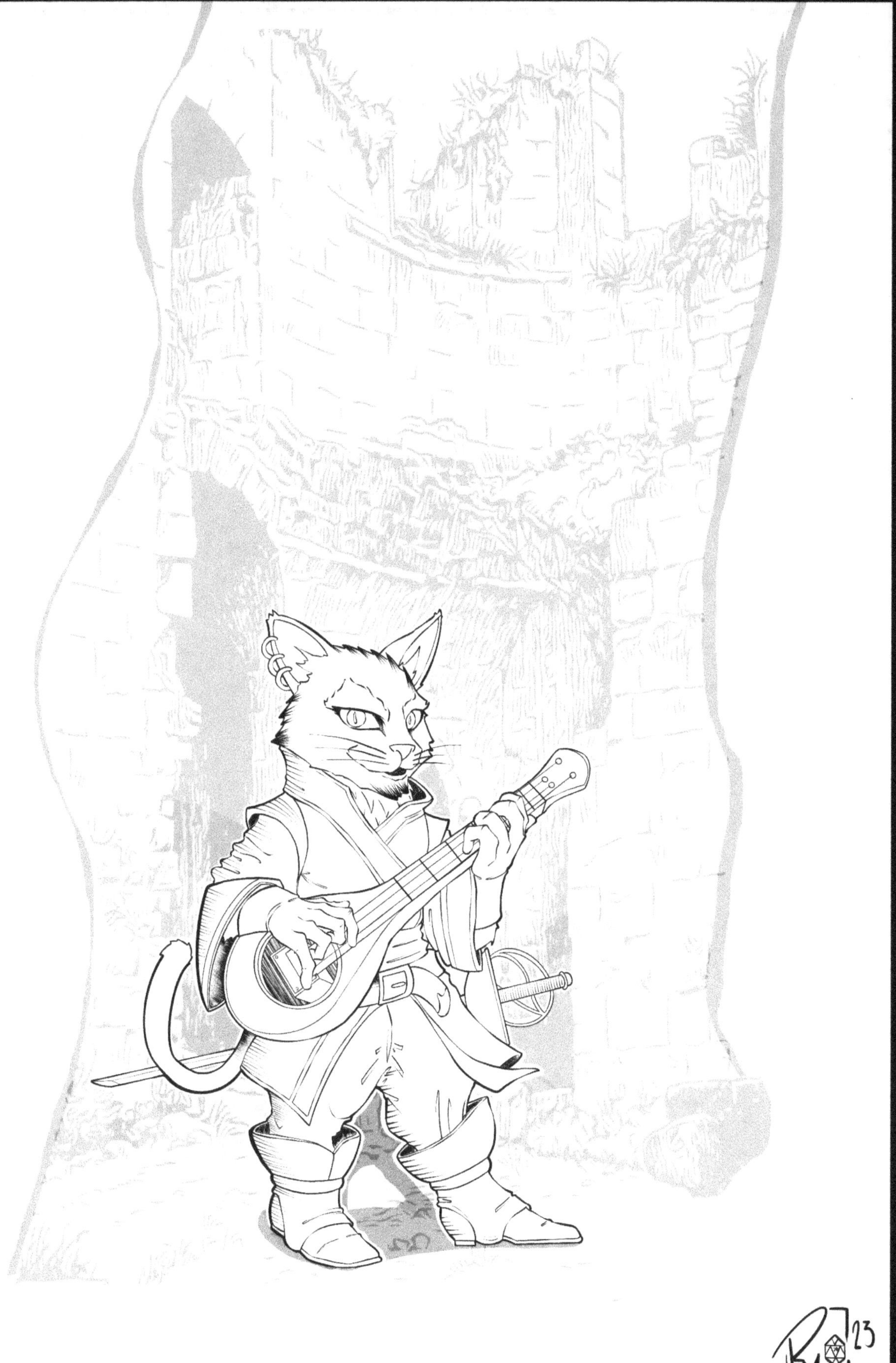

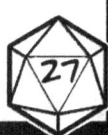

ON THIS PAGE, YOU CAN WRITE DOWN ANY RELEVANT MATTER OF THE STORY AND ADVENTURES THAT YOUR CHARACTER LIVES: THE CLUE ABOUT A TREASURE, THE MAP OF A DUNGEON, RUMORS ABOUT THE WHEREABOUTS OF A RELEVANT PERSON... IT'S YOUR ADVENTURE, MAKE IT EPIC!

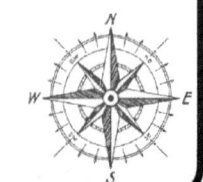

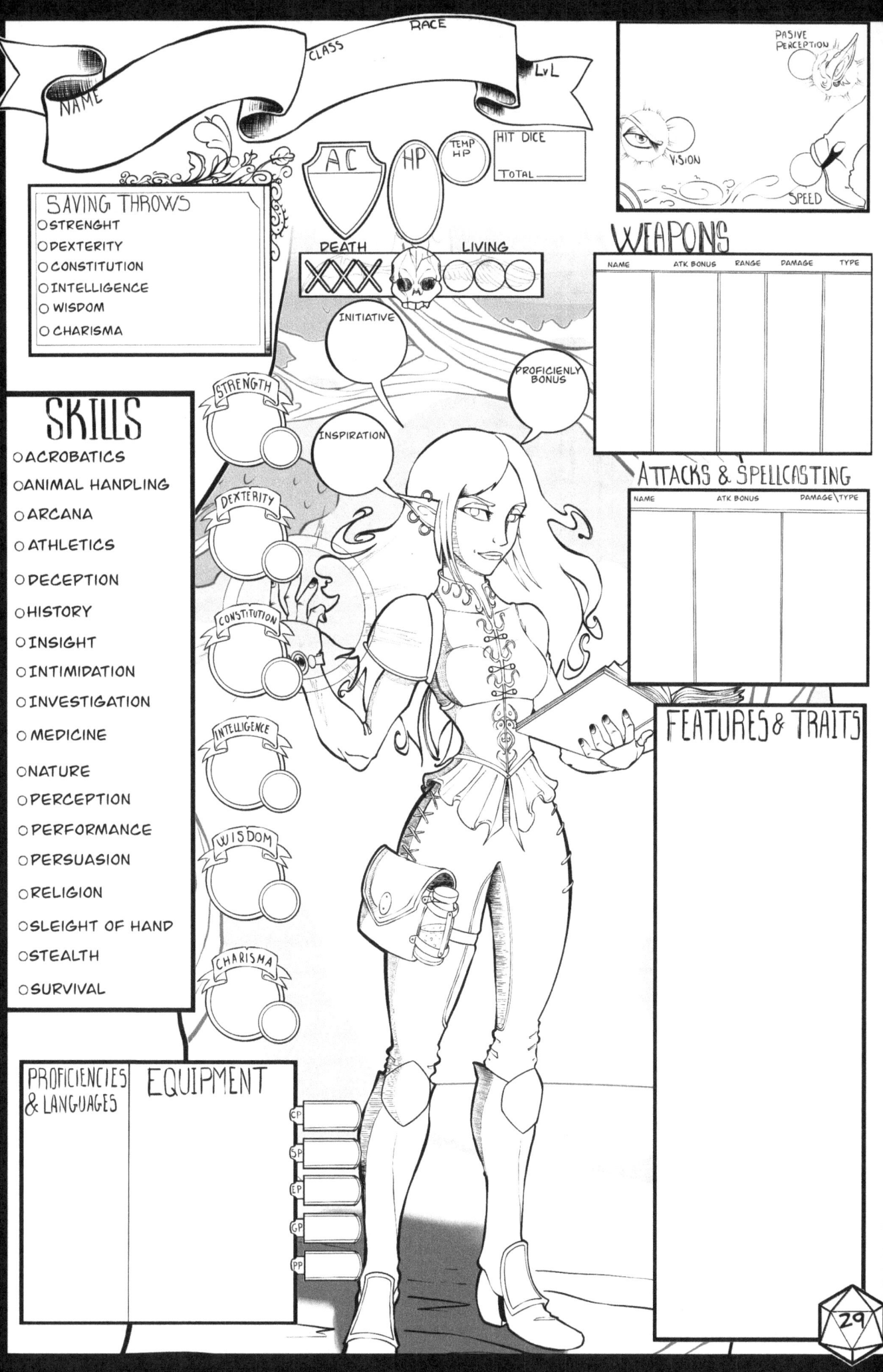

NAME

CLASS RACE LvL

PASIVE PERCEPTION

VISION SPEED

AC HP TEMP HP

HIT DICE
TOTAL ____

SAVING THROWS
- STRENGHT
- DEXTERITY
- CONSTITUTION
- INTELLIGENCE
- WISDOM
- CHARISMA

DEATH LIVING

INITIATIVE

PROFICIENLY BONUS

INSPIRATION

WEAPONS

NAME	ATK BONUS	RANGE	DAMAGE	TYPE

ATTACKS & SPELLCASTING

NAME	ATK BONUS	DAMAGE\TYPE

SKILLS
- ACROBATICS
- ANIMAL HANDLING
- ARCANA
- ATHLETICS
- DECEPTION
- HISTORY
- INSIGHT
- INTIMIDATION
- INVESTIGATION
- MEDICINE
- NATURE
- PERCEPTION
- PERFORMANCE
- PERSUASION
- RELIGION
- SLEIGHT OF HAND
- STEALTH
- SURVIVAL

STRENGTH

DEXTERITY

CONSTITUTION

INTELLIGENCE

WISDOM

CHARISMA

FEATURES & TRAITS

PROFICIENCIES & LANGUAGES

EQUIPMENT

CP
SP
EP
GP
PP

29

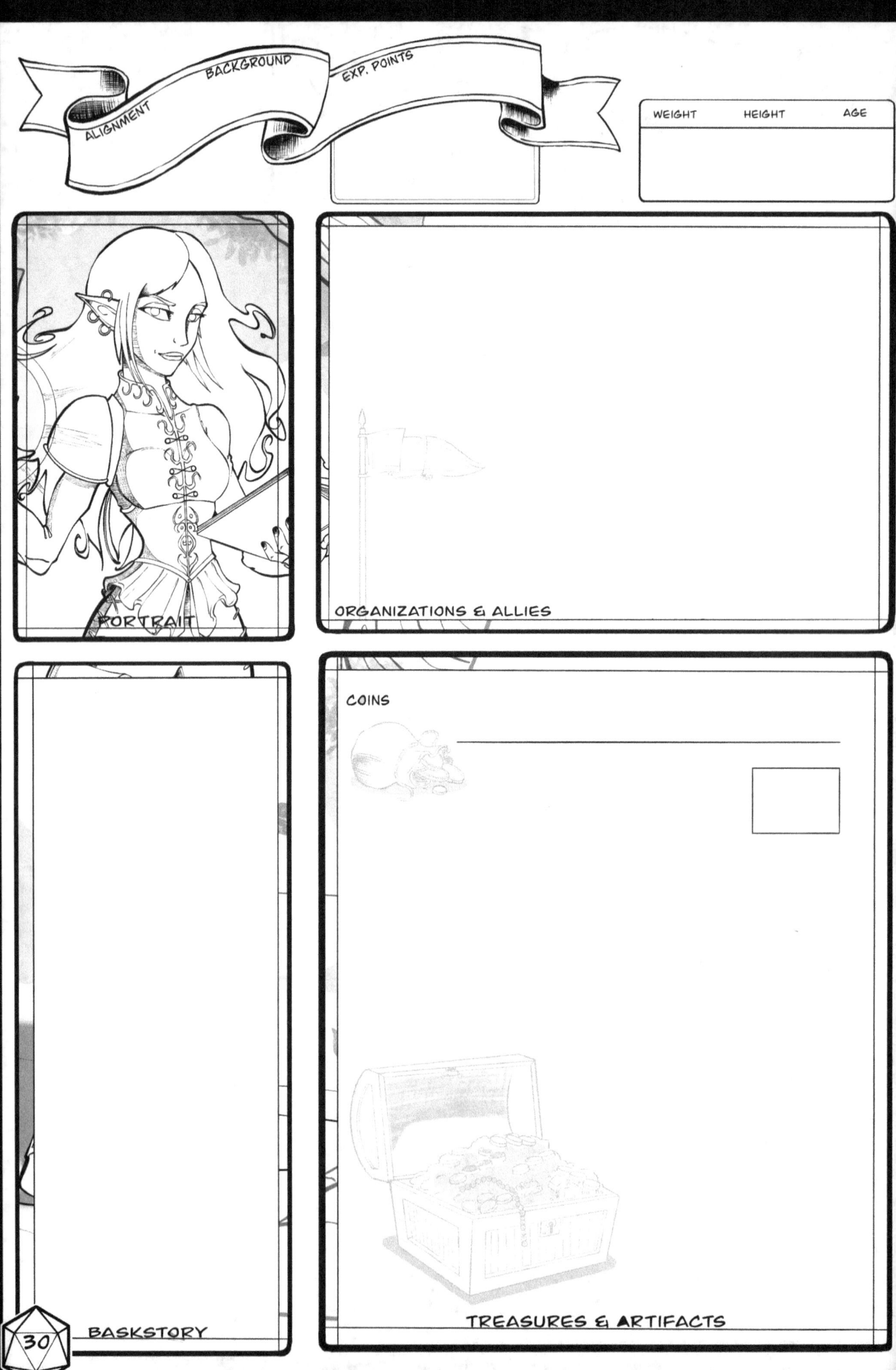

ALIGNMENT BACKGROUND EXP. POINTS

WEIGHT HEIGHT AGE

PORTRAIT

ORGANIZATIONS & ALLIES

COINS

BASKSTORY

TREASURES & ARTIFACTS

30

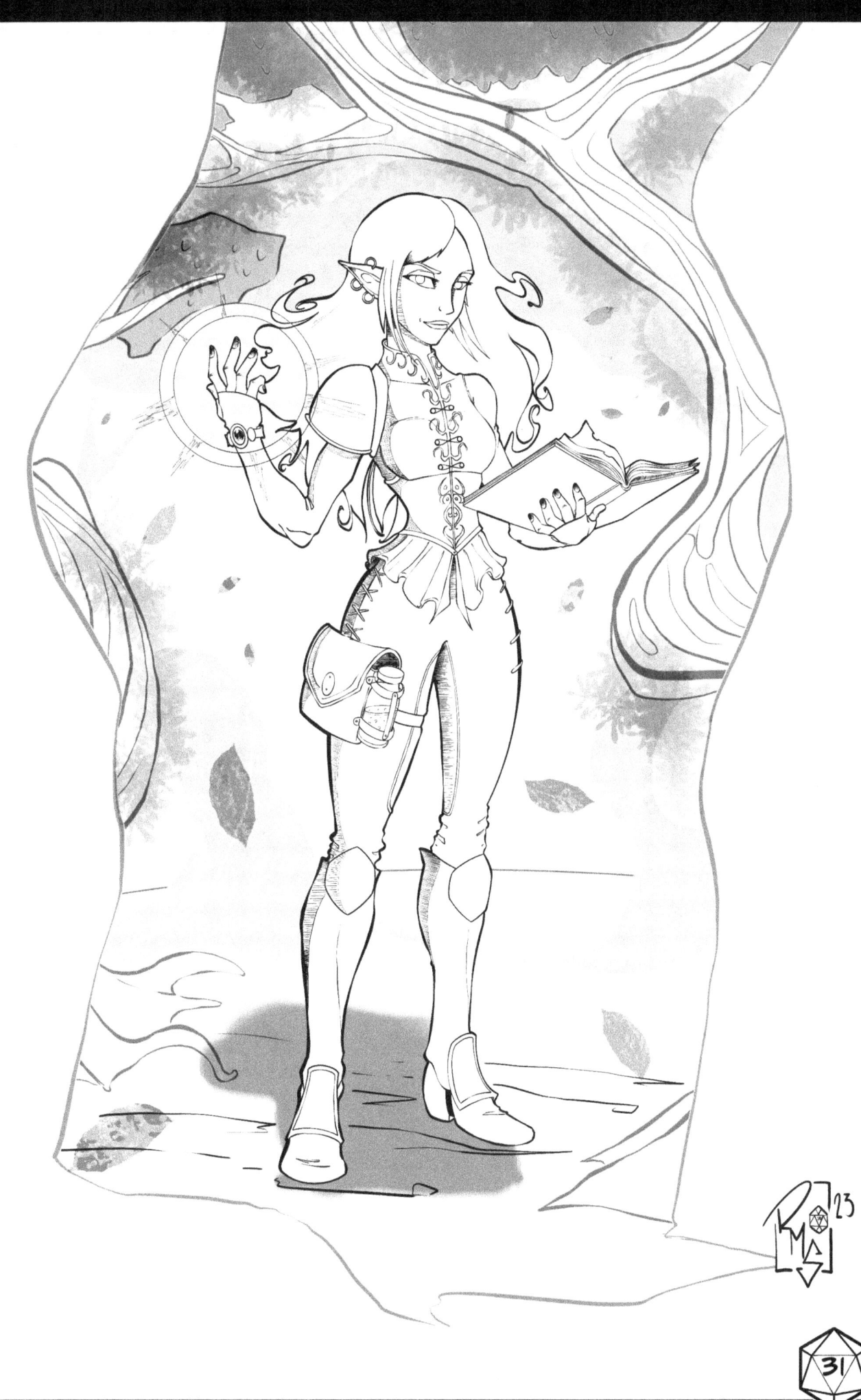

ON THIS PAGE, YOU CAN WRITE DOWN ANY RELEVANT MATTER OF THE STORY AND ADVENTURES THAT YOUR CHARACTER LIVES: THE CLUE ABOUT A TREASURE, THE MAP OF A DUNGEON, RUMORS ABOUT THE WHEREABOUTS OF A RELEVANT PERSON... IT'S YOUR ADVENTURE, MAKE IT EPIC!

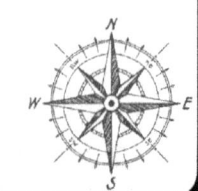

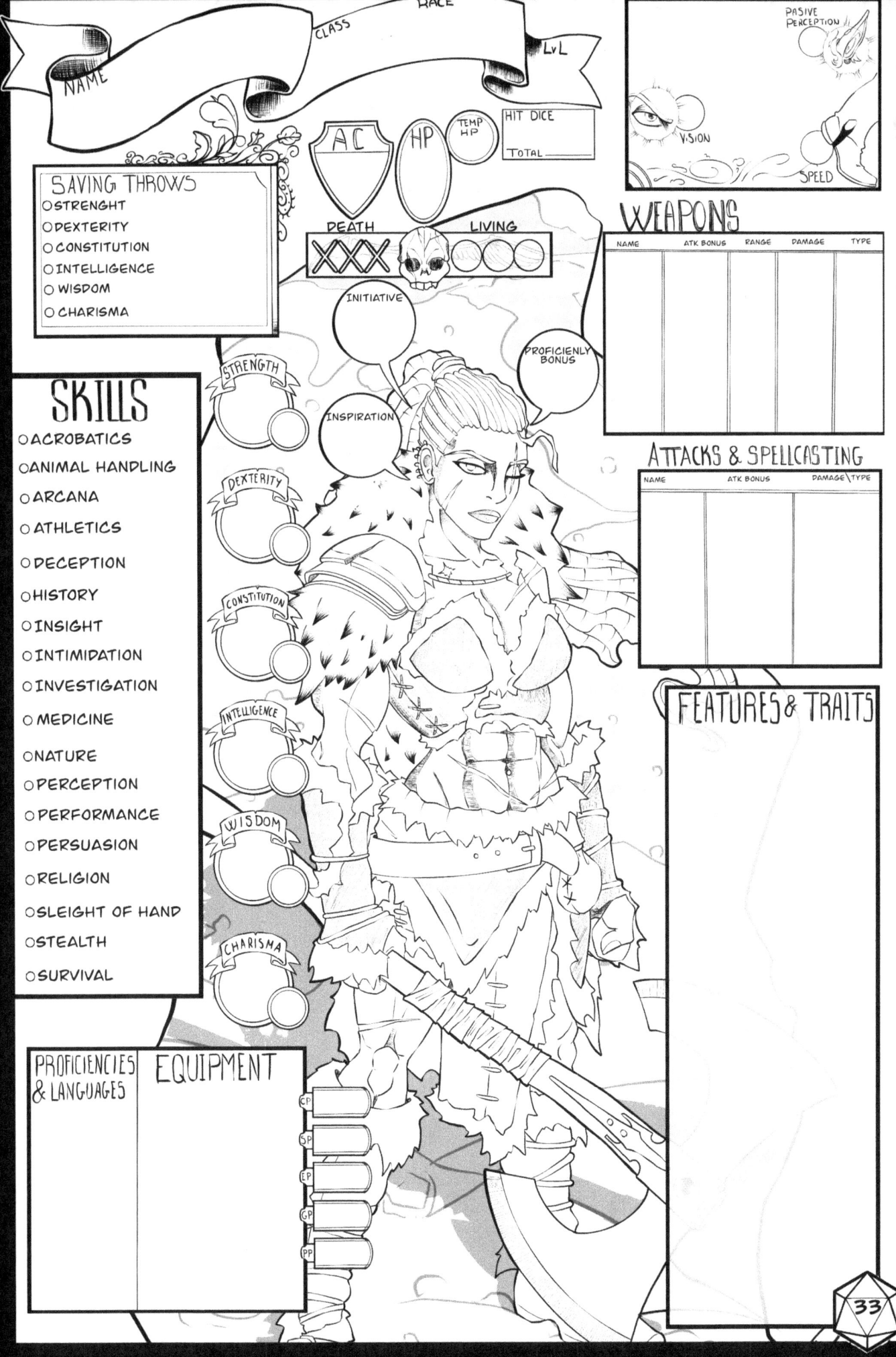

CLASS
RACE
LvL

NAME

PASIVE PERCEPTION

AC
HP
TEMP HP

HIT DICE

TOTAL _____

VISION

SPEED

SAVING THROWS
- ○ STRENGHT
- ○ DEXTERITY
- ○ CONSTITUTION
- ○ INTELLIGENCE
- ○ WISDOM
- ○ CHARISMA

DEATH LIVING

XXX

INITIATIVE

PROFICIENLY BONUS

WEAPONS

NAME	ATK BONUS	RANGE	DAMAGE	TYPE

STRENGTH

INSPIRATION

SKILLS
- ○ ACROBATICS
- ○ ANIMAL HANDLING
- ○ ARCANA
- ○ ATHLETICS
- ○ DECEPTION
- ○ HISTORY
- ○ INSIGHT
- ○ INTIMIDATION
- ○ INVESTIGATION
- ○ MEDICINE
- ○ NATURE
- ○ PERCEPTION
- ○ PERFORMANCE
- ○ PERSUASION
- ○ RELIGION
- ○ SLEIGHT OF HAND
- ○ STEALTH
- ○ SURVIVAL

DEXTERITY

CONSTITUTION

INTELLIGENCE

WISDOM

CHARISMA

ATTACKS & SPELLCASTING

NAME	ATK BONUS	DAMAGE\TYPE

FEATURES & TRAITS

PROFICIENCIES & LANGUAGES

EQUIPMENT

CP
SP
EP
GP
PP

33

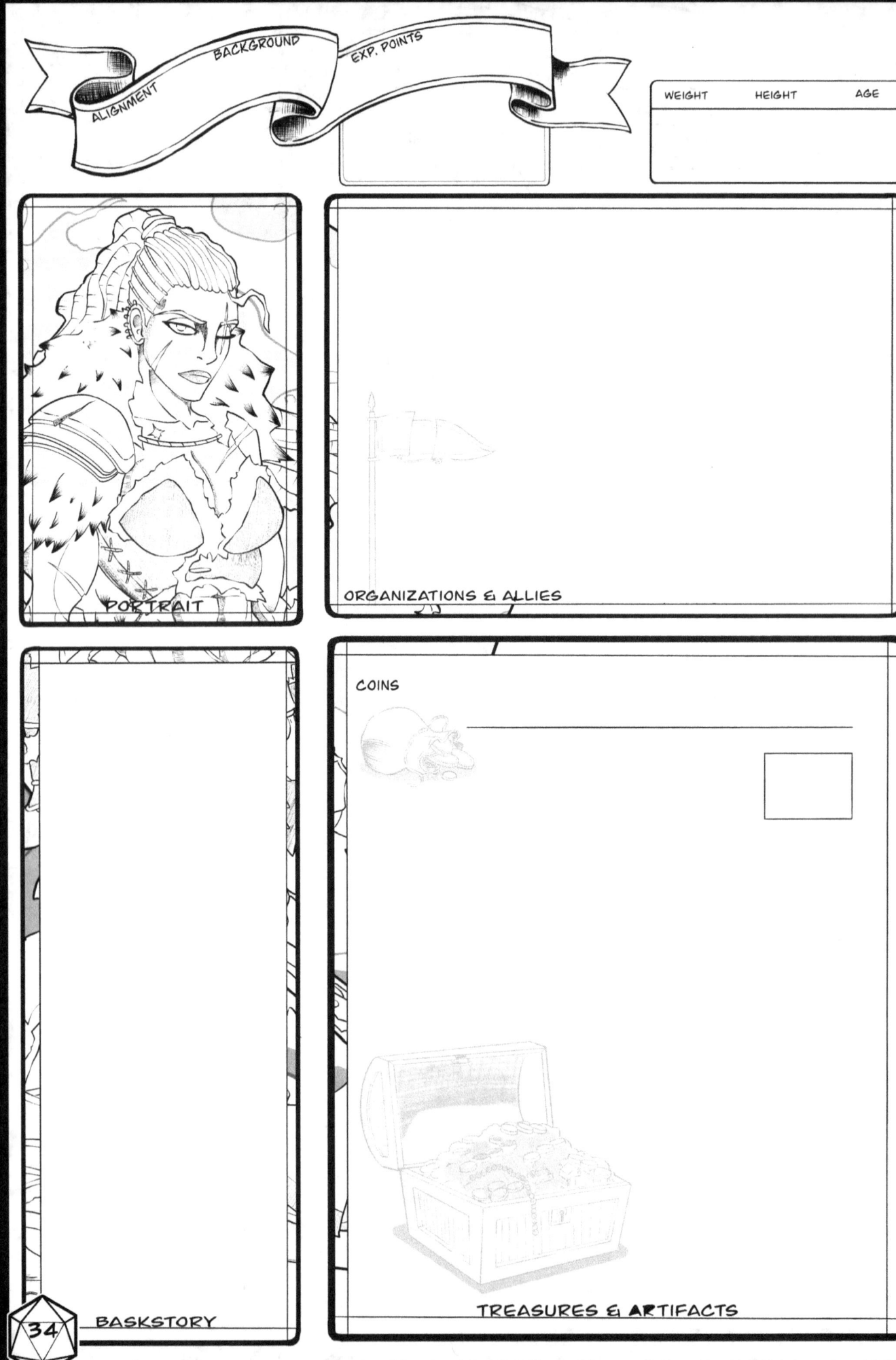

ALIGNMENT BACKGROUND EXP. POINTS

WEIGHT   HEIGHT   AGE

PORTRAIT

ORGANIZATIONS & ALLIES

COINS

BASKSTORY

TREASURES & ARTIFACTS

34

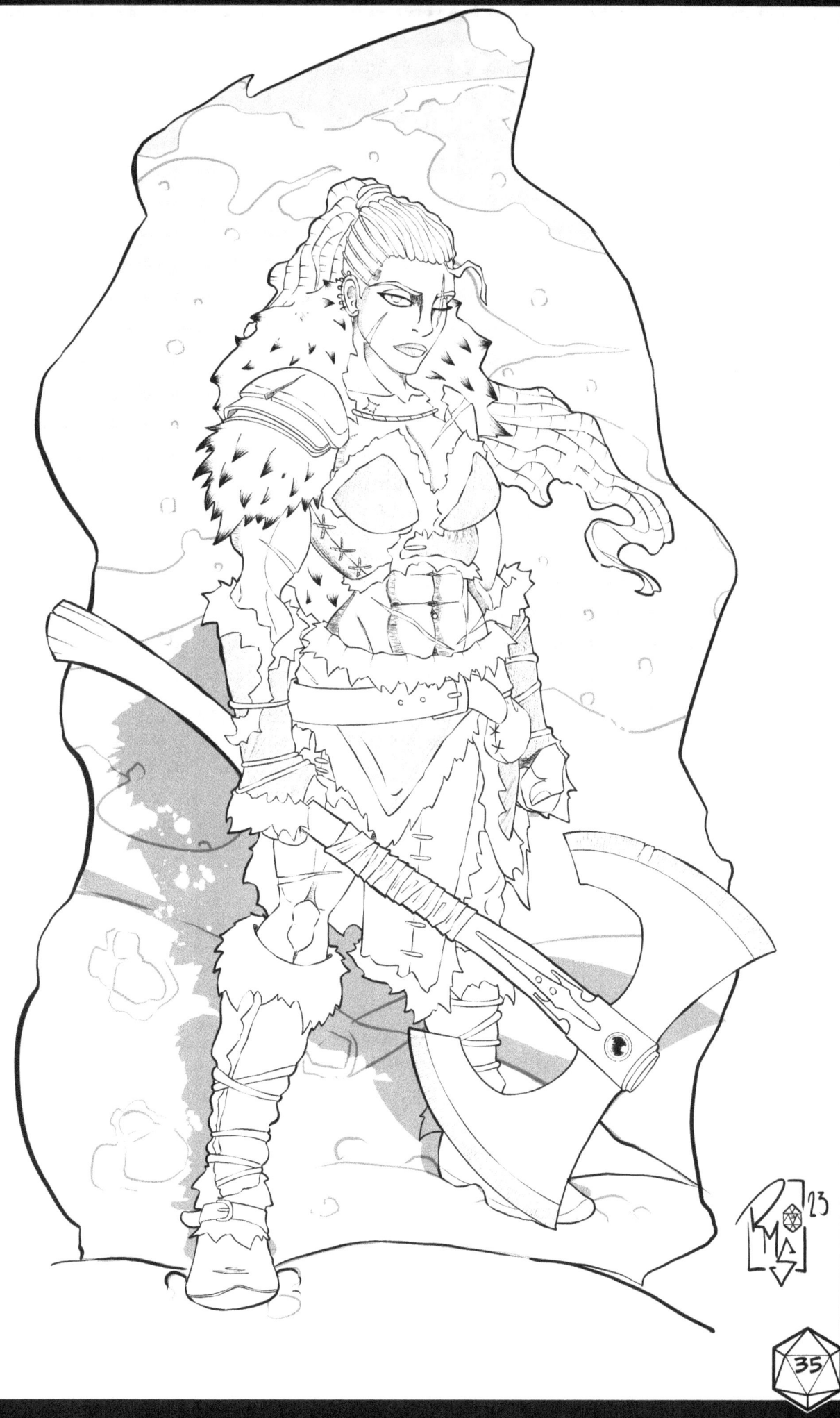

ON THIS PAGE, YOU CAN WRITE DOWN ANY RELEVANT MATTER OF THE STORY AND ADVENTURES THAT YOUR CHARACTER LIVES: THE CLUE ABOUT A TREASURE, THE MAP OF A DUNGEON, RUMORS ABOUT THE WHEREABOUTS OF A RELEVANT PERSON... IT'S YOUR ADVENTURE, MAKE IT EPIC!

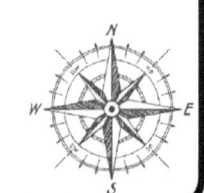

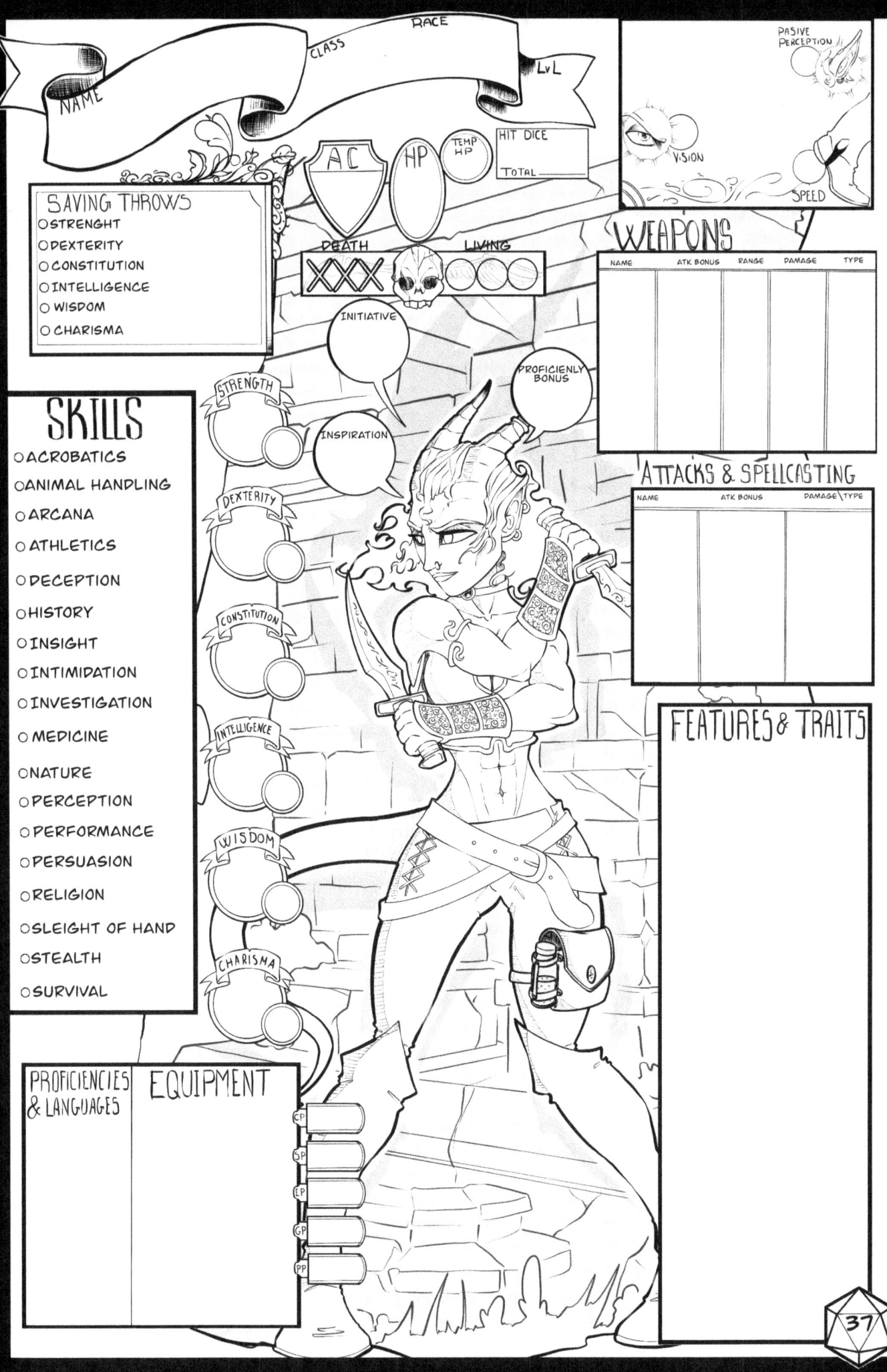

NAME

CLASS RACE LvL

AC HP TEMP HP

HIT DICE
TOTAL

PASIVE PERCEPTION

VISION SPEED

SAVING THROWS
- O STRENGHT
- O DEXTERITY
- O CONSTITUTION
- O INTELLIGENCE
- O WISDOM
- O CHARISMA

DEATH XXX LIVING

INITIATIVE

INSPIRATION

PROFICIENLY BONUS

WEAPONS
NAME	ATK BONUS	RANGE	DAMAGE	TYPE

ATTACKS & SPELLCASTING
NAME	ATK BONUS	DAMAGE\TYPE

SKILLS
- O ACROBATICS
- O ANIMAL HANDLING
- O ARCANA
- O ATHLETICS
- O DECEPTION
- O HISTORY
- O INSIGHT
- O INTIMIDATION
- O INVESTIGATION
- O MEDICINE
- O NATURE
- O PERCEPTION
- O PERFORMANCE
- O PERSUASION
- O RELIGION
- O SLEIGHT OF HAND
- O STEALTH
- O SURVIVAL

STRENGTH

DEXTERITY

CONSTITUTION

INTELLIGENCE

WISDOM

CHARISMA

FEATURES & TRAITS

PROFICIENCIES & LANGUAGES

EQUIPMENT

CP
SP
EP
GP
PP

37

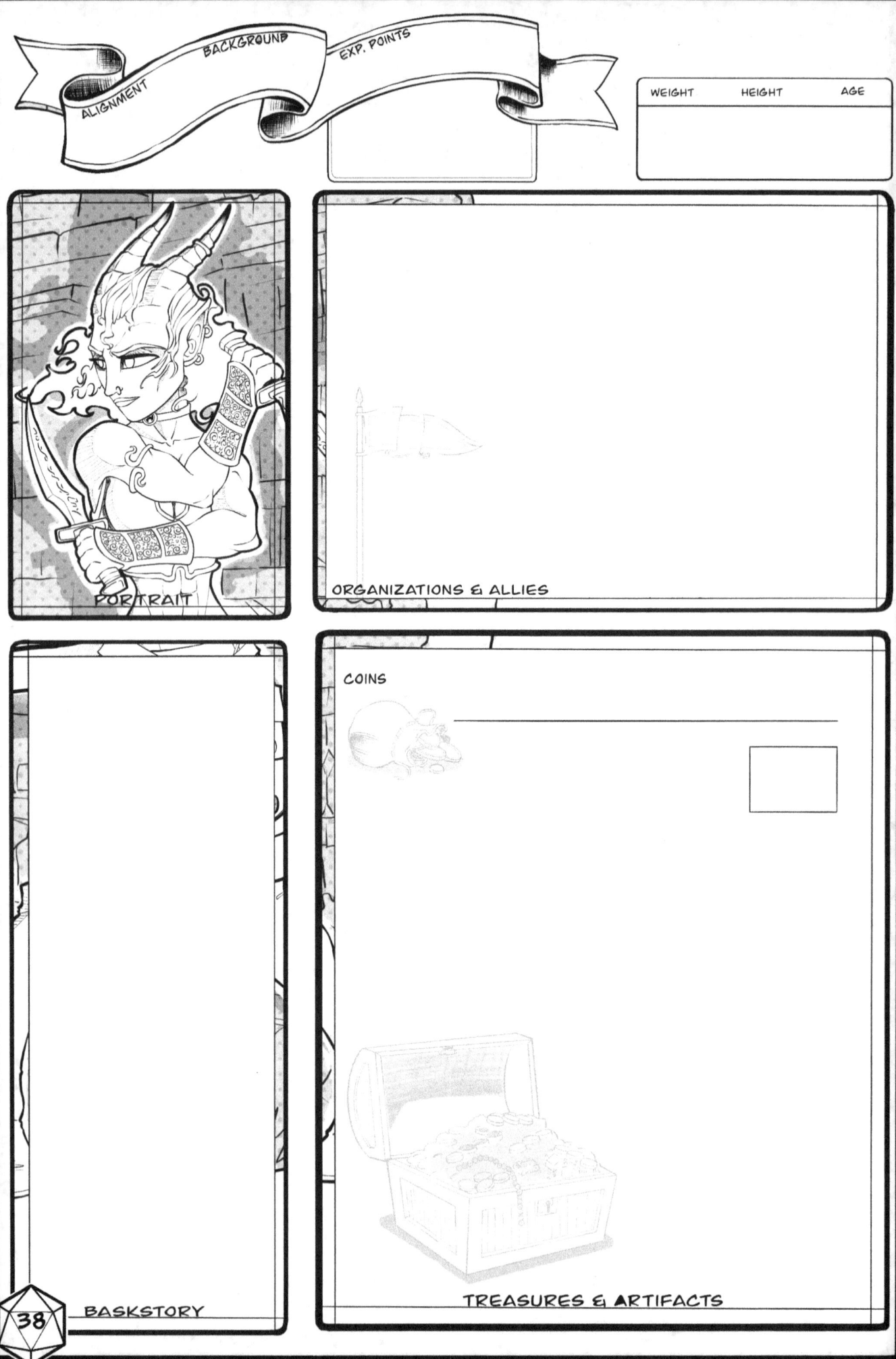

ALIGNMENT   BACKGROUND   EXP. POINTS

WEIGHT   HEIGHT   AGE

PORTRAIT

ORGANIZATIONS & ALLIES

COINS

BASKSTORY

TREASURES & ARTIFACTS

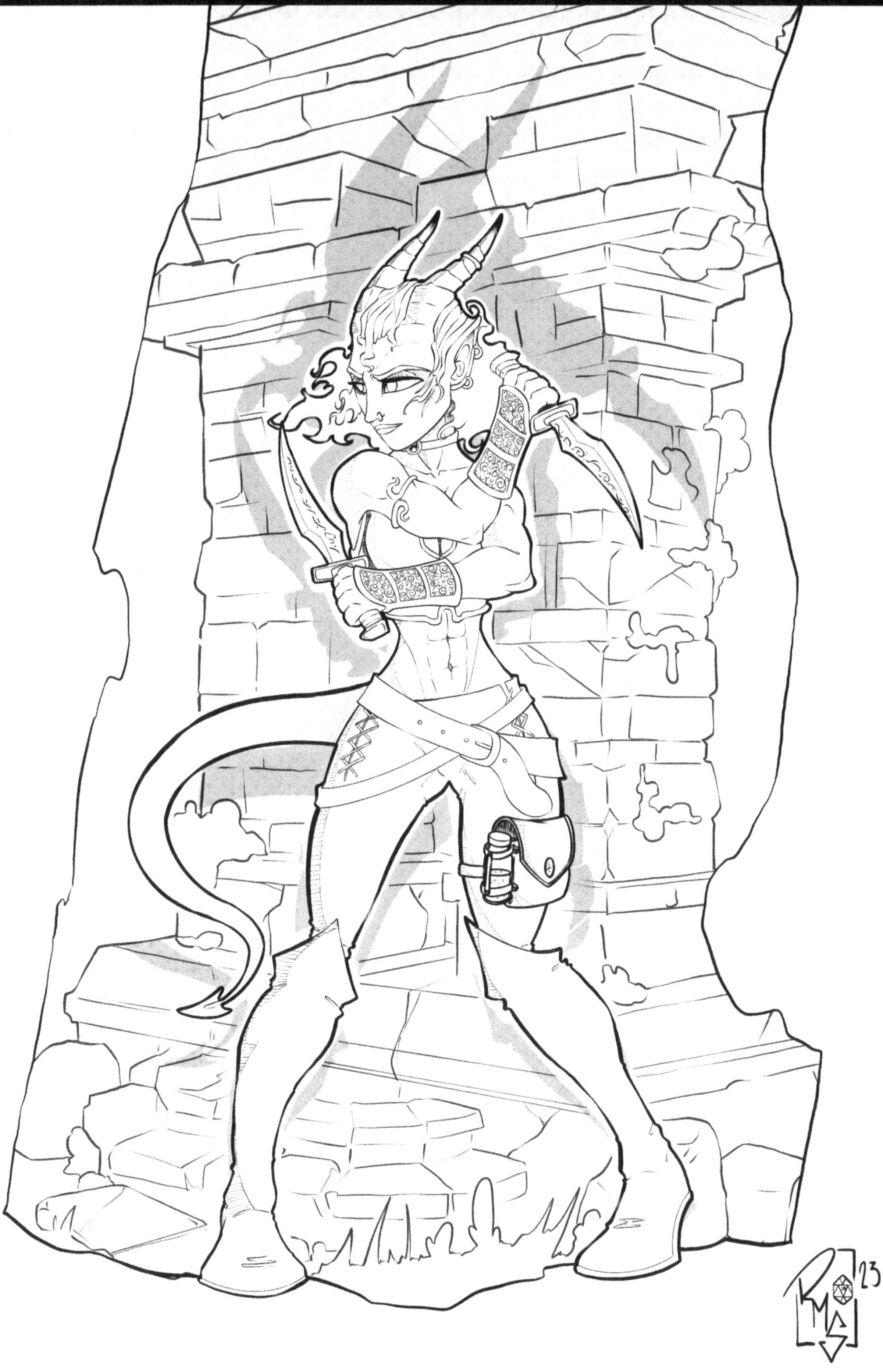

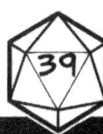

ON THIS PAGE, YOU CAN WRITE DOWN ANY RELEVANT MATTER OF THE STORY AND ADVENTURES THAT YOUR CHARACTER LIVES: THE CLUE ABOUT A TREASURE, THE MAP OF A DUNGEON, RUMORS ABOUT THE WHEREABOUTS OF A RELEVANT PERSON... IT'S YOUR ADVENTURE, MAKE IT EPIC!

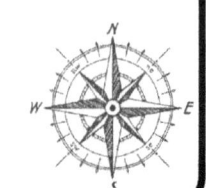

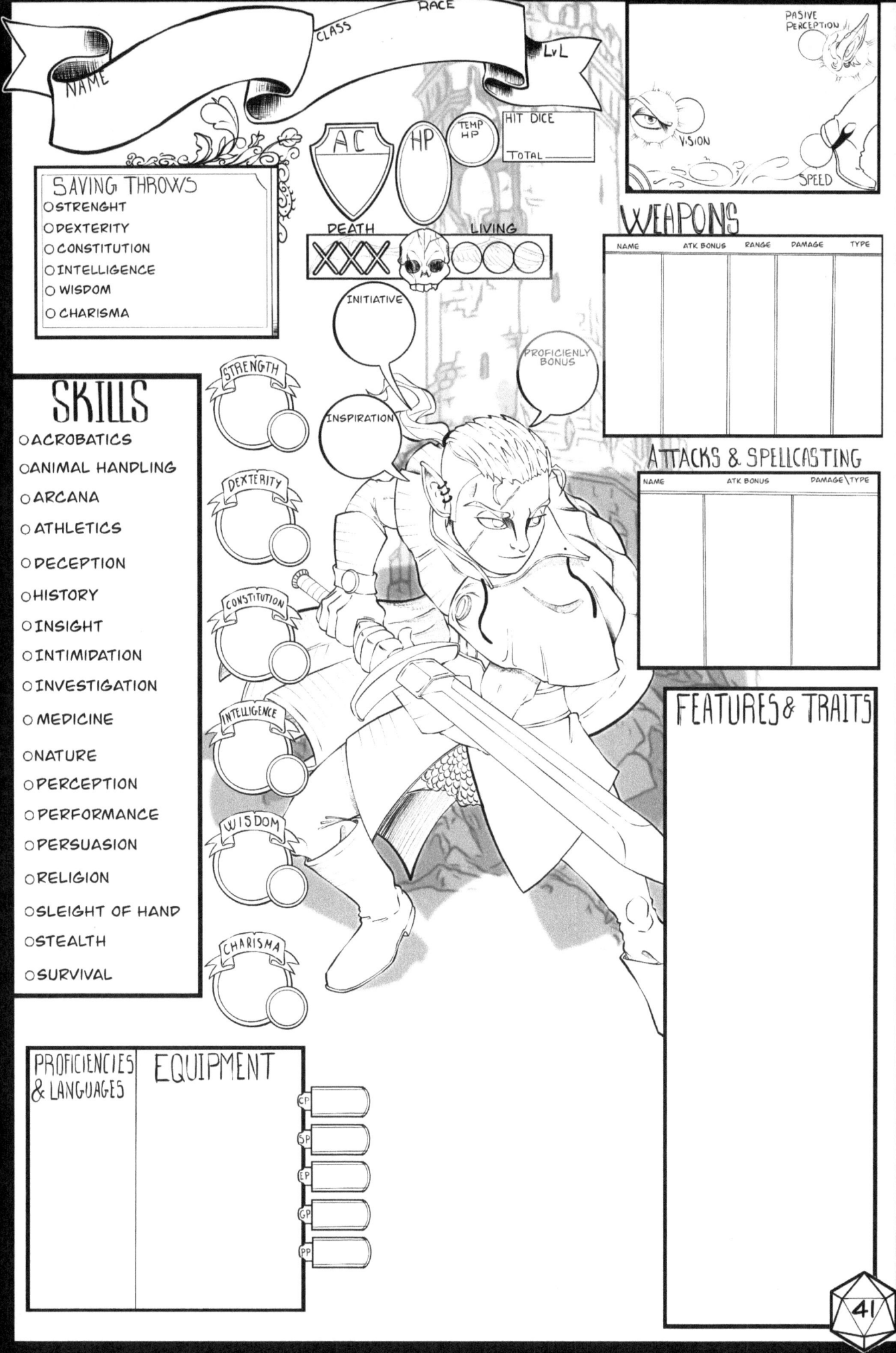

NAME

CLASS RACE LvL

AC HP TEMP HP

HIT DICE
TOTAL _____

PASIVE PERCEPTION

VISION SPEED

DEATH LIVING

INITIATIVE

PROFICIENLY BONUS

INSPIRATION

SAVING THROWS
- ○ STRENGHT
- ○ DEXTERITY
- ○ CONSTITUTION
- ○ INTELLIGENCE
- ○ WISDOM
- ○ CHARISMA

SKILLS
- ○ ACROBATICS
- ○ ANIMAL HANDLING
- ○ ARCANA
- ○ ATHLETICS
- ○ DECEPTION
- ○ HISTORY
- ○ INSIGHT
- ○ INTIMIDATION
- ○ INVESTIGATION
- ○ MEDICINE
- ○ NATURE
- ○ PERCEPTION
- ○ PERFORMANCE
- ○ PERSUASION
- ○ RELIGION
- ○ SLEIGHT OF HAND
- ○ STEALTH
- ○ SURVIVAL

STRENGTH

DEXTERITY

CONSTITUTION

INTELLIGENCE

WISDOM

CHARISMA

WEAPONS

NAME	ATK BONUS	RANGE	DAMAGE	TYPE

ATTACKS & SPELLCASTING

NAME	ATK BONUS	DAMAGE\TYPE

FEATURES & TRAITS

PROFICIENCIES & LANGUAGES

EQUIPMENT

CP
SP
EP
GP
PP

41

ALIGNMENT   BACKGROUND   EXP. POINTS

WEIGHT   HEIGHT   AGE

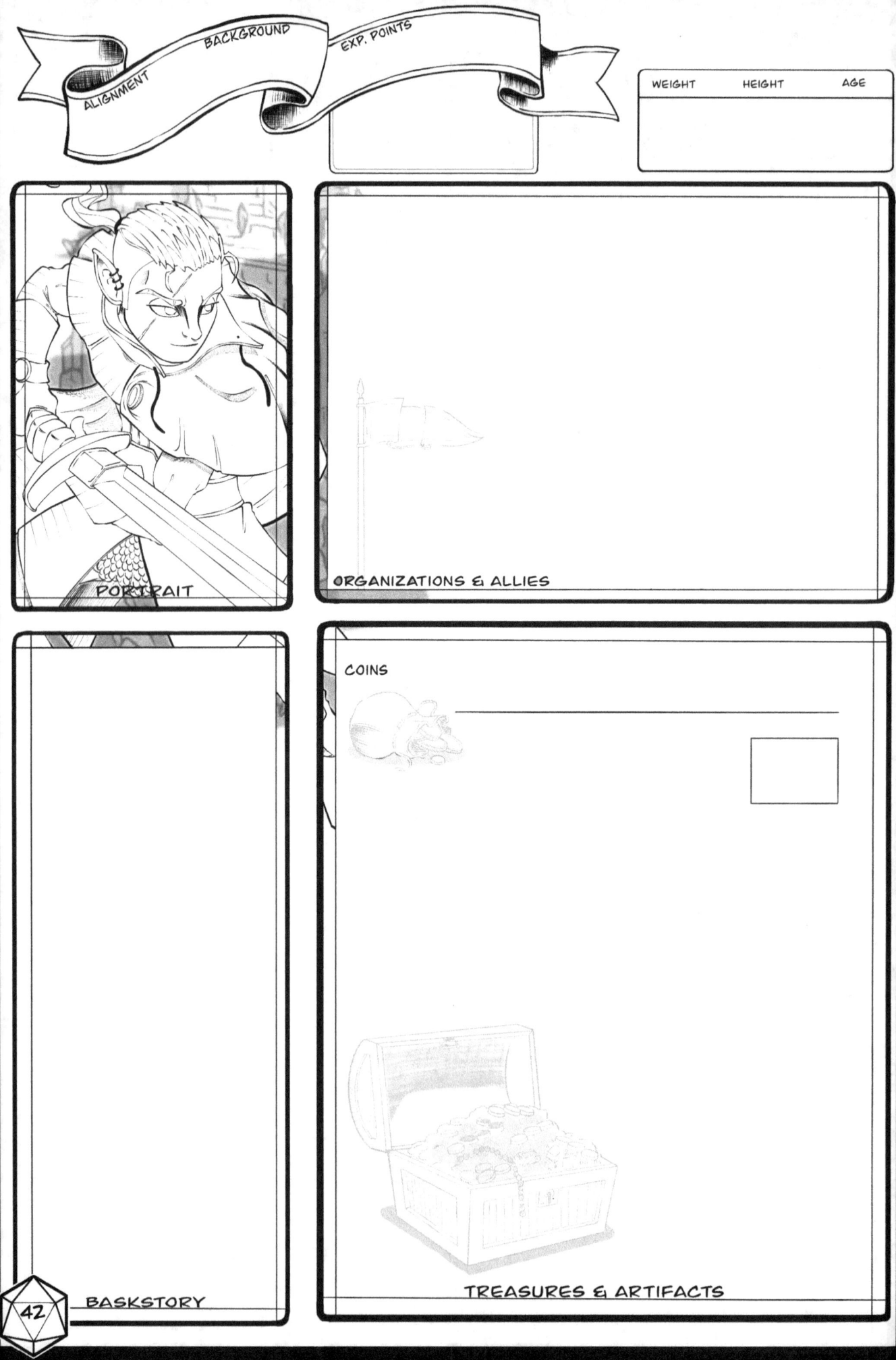

PORTRAIT

ORGANIZATIONS & ALLIES

COINS

BASKSTORY

TREASURES & ARTIFACTS

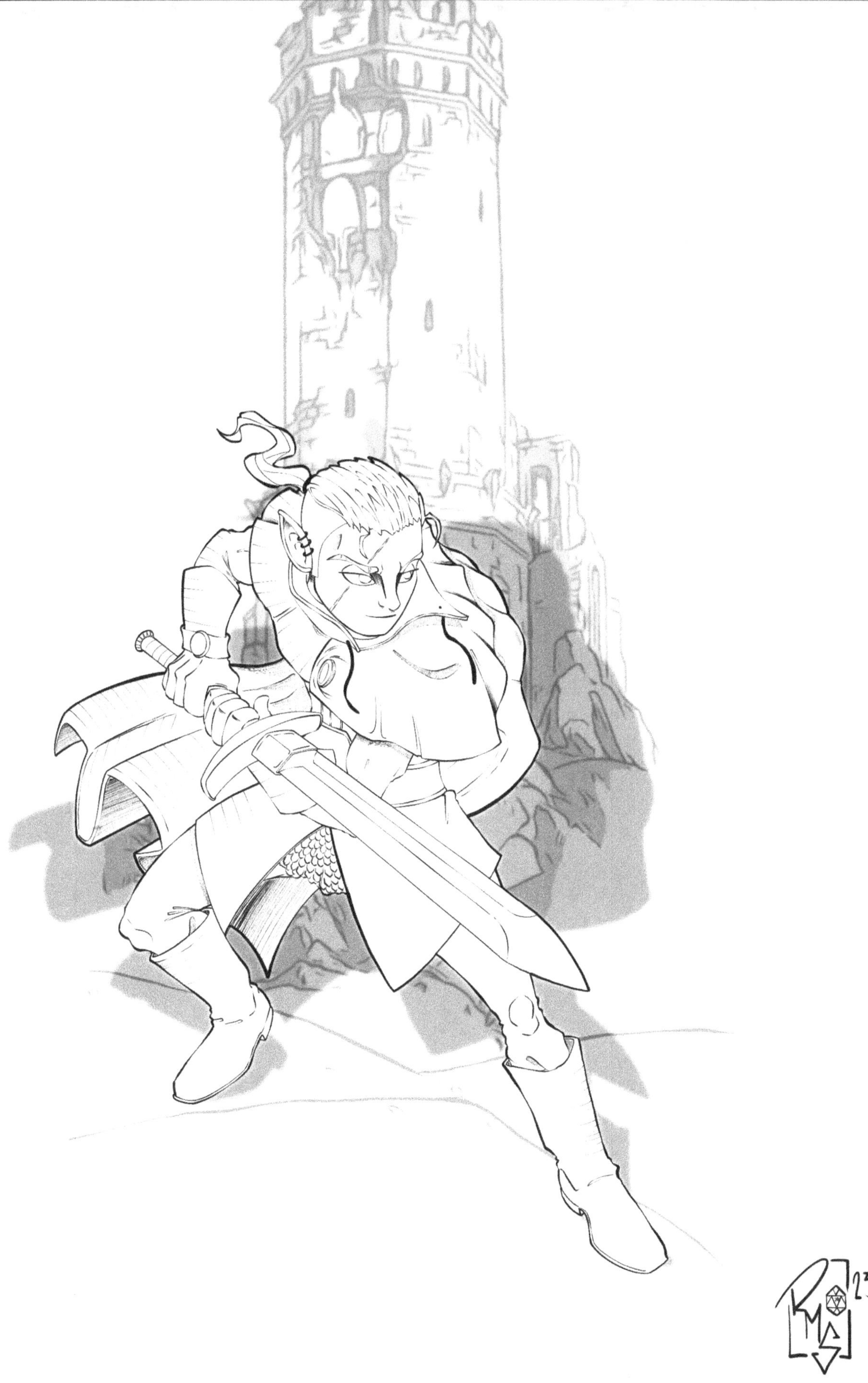

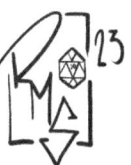
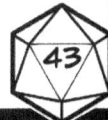

ON THIS PAGE, YOU CAN WRITE DOWN ANY RELEVANT MATTER OF THE STORY AND ADVENTURES THAT YOUR CHARACTER LIVES: THE CLUE ABOUT A TREASURE, THE MAP OF A DUNGEON, RUMORS ABOUT THE WHEREABOUTS OF A RELEVANT PERSON... IT'S YOUR ADVENTURE, MAKE IT EPIC!

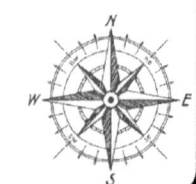

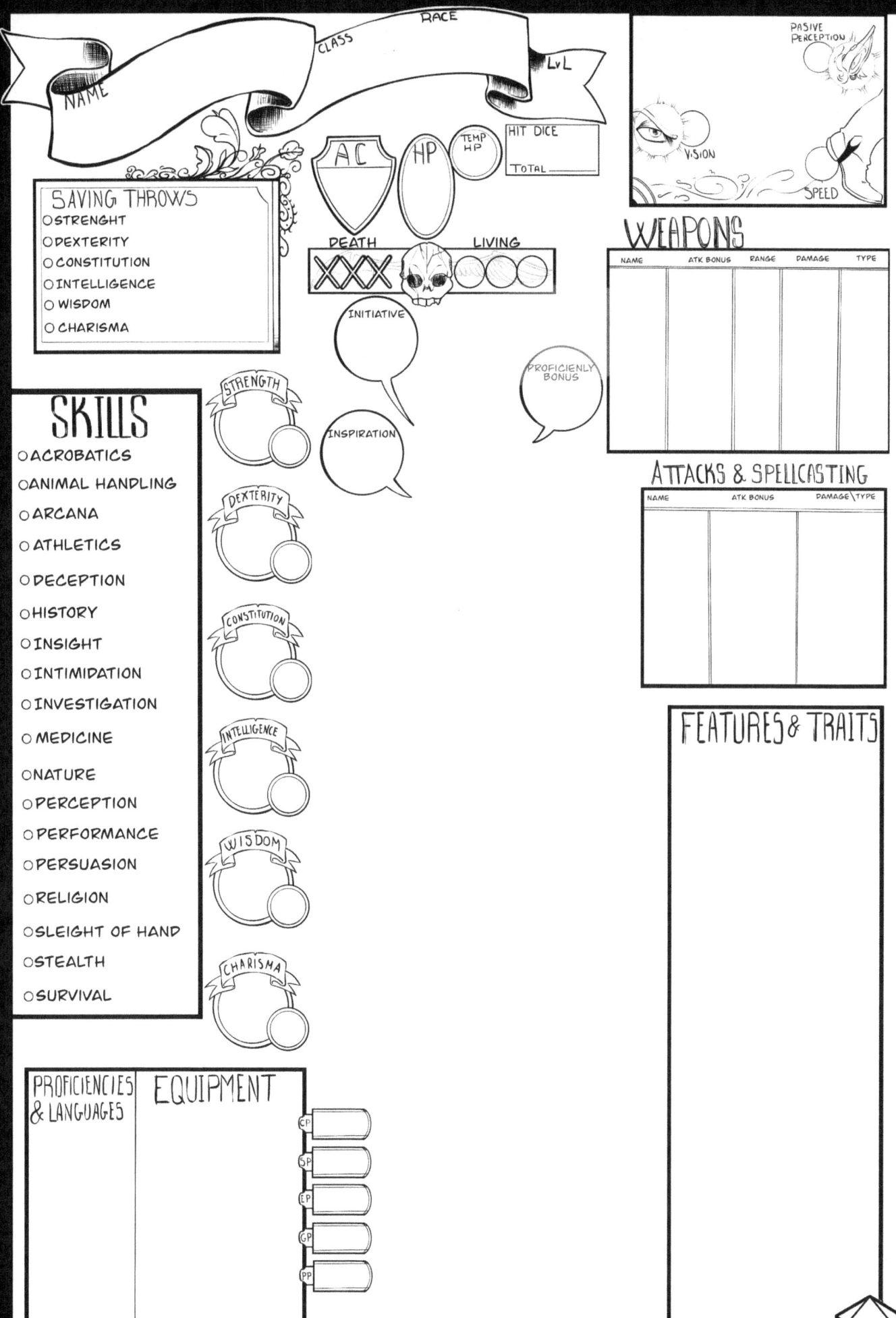

NAME
CLASS
RACE
LvL

AC HP TEMP HP

HIT DICE
TOTAL _____

PASIVE PERCEPTION

VISION
SPEED

SAVING THROWS
- O STRENGHT
- O DEXTERITY
- O CONSTITUTION
- O INTELLIGENCE
- O WISDOM
- O CHARISMA

DEATH ✗✗✗ LIVING

INITIATIVE

INSPIRATION

PROFICIENLY BONUS

WEAPONS

NAME	ATK BONUS	RANGE	DAMAGE	TYPE

ATTACKS & SPELLCASTING

NAME	ATK BONUS	DAMAGE\TYPE

SKILLS
- O ACROBATICS
- O ANIMAL HANDLING
- O ARCANA
- O ATHLETICS
- O DECEPTION
- O HISTORY
- O INSIGHT
- O INTIMIDATION
- O INVESTIGATION
- O MEDICINE
- O NATURE
- O PERCEPTION
- O PERFORMANCE
- O PERSUASION
- O RELIGION
- O SLEIGHT OF HAND
- O STEALTH
- O SURVIVAL

STRENGTH

DEXTERITY

CONSTITUTION

INTELLIGENCE

WISDOM

CHARISMA

FEATURES & TRAITS

PROFICIENCIES & LANGUAGES

EQUIPMENT

CP
SP
EP
GP
PP

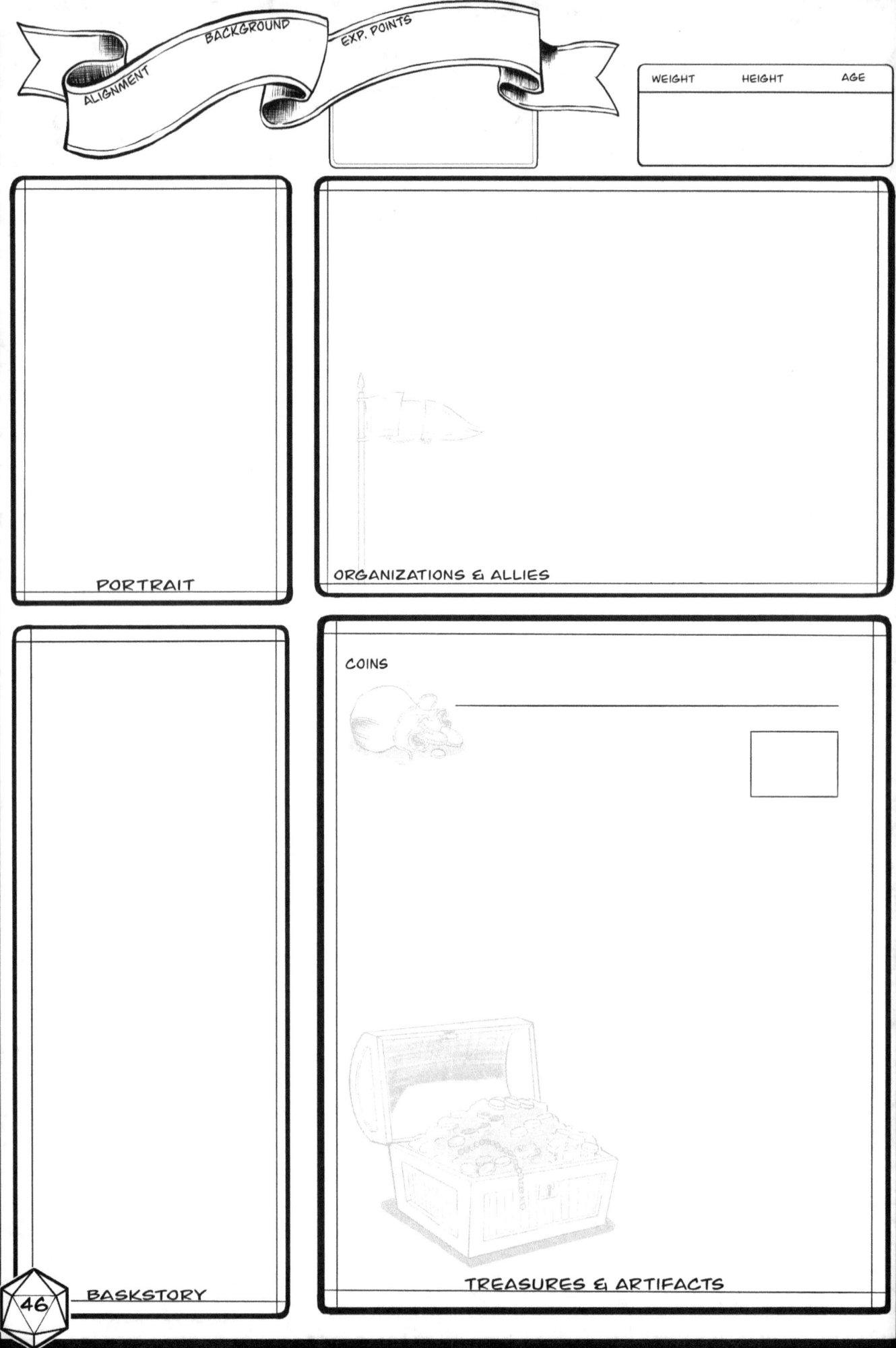

ALIGNMENT

BACKGROUND

EXP. POINTS

WEIGHT   HEIGHT   AGE

PORTRAIT

ORGANIZATIONS & ALLIES

COINS

BASKSTORY

TREASURES & ARTIFACTS

46

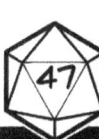

ON THIS PAGE, YOU CAN WRITE DOWN ANY RELEVANT MATTER OF THE STORY AND ADVENTURES THAT YOUR CHARACTER LIVES: THE CLUE ABOUT A TREASURE, THE MAP OF A DUNGEON, RUMORS ABOUT THE WHEREABOUTS OF A RELEVANT PERSON... IT'S YOUR ADVENTURE, MAKE IT EPIC!

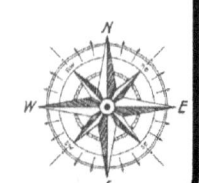

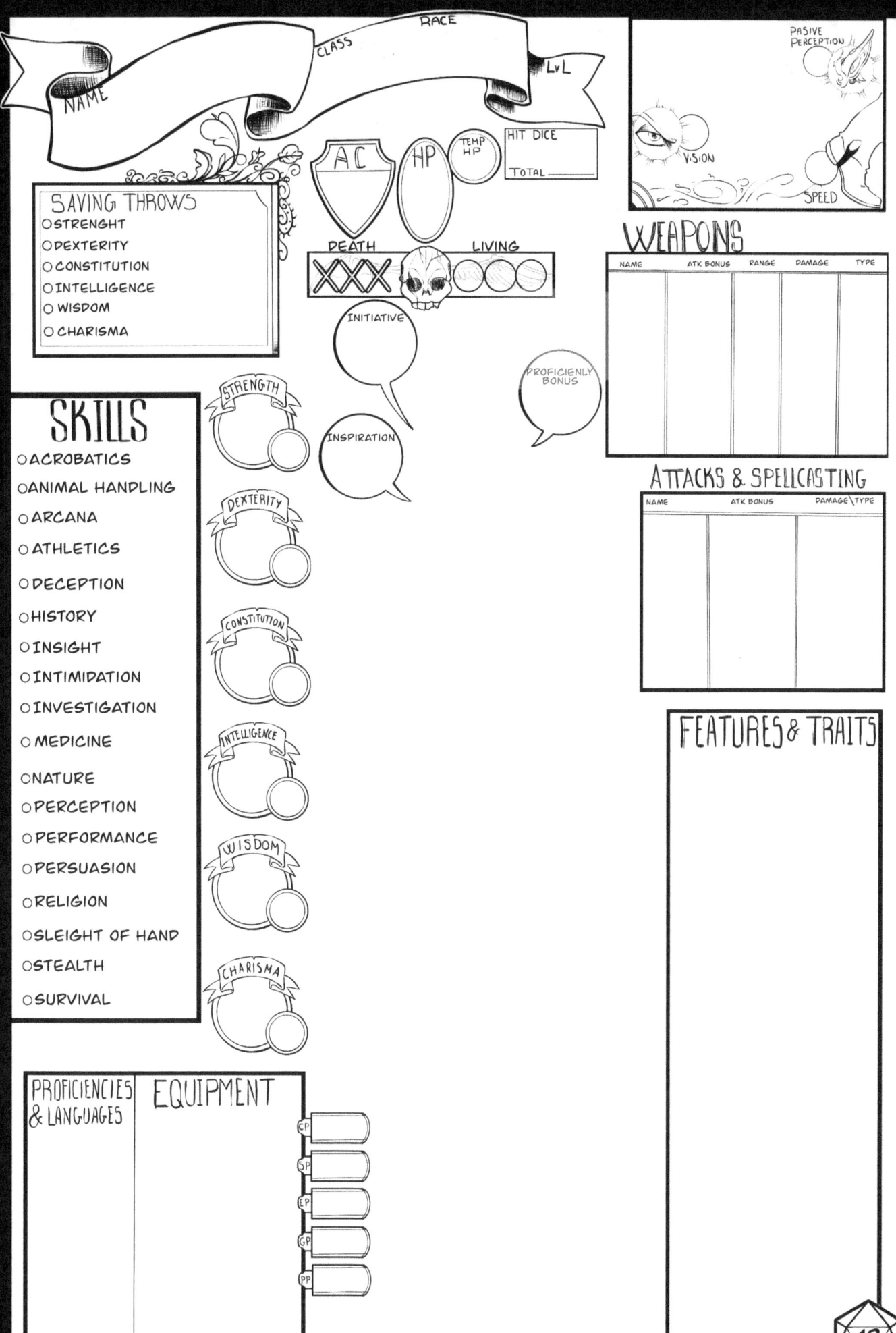

NAME

CLASS   RACE   LvL

AC   HP   TEMP HP

HIT DICE
TOTAL _____

PASIVE PERCEPTION

VISION

SPEED

SAVING THROWS
- ○ STRENGHT
- ○ DEXTERITY
- ○ CONSTITUTION
- ○ INTELLIGENCE
- ○ WISDOM
- ○ CHARISMA

DEATH   LIVING

INITIATIVE

INSPIRATION

PROFICIENLY BONUS

WEAPONS

NAME	ATK BONUS	RANGE	DAMAGE	TYPE

SKILLS
- ○ ACROBATICS
- ○ ANIMAL HANDLING
- ○ ARCANA
- ○ ATHLETICS
- ○ DECEPTION
- ○ HISTORY
- ○ INSIGHT
- ○ INTIMIDATION
- ○ INVESTIGATION
- ○ MEDICINE
- ○ NATURE
- ○ PERCEPTION
- ○ PERFORMANCE
- ○ PERSUASION
- ○ RELIGION
- ○ SLEIGHT OF HAND
- ○ STEALTH
- ○ SURVIVAL

STRENGTH

DEXTERITY

CONSTITUTION

INTELLIGENCE

WISDOM

CHARISMA

ATTACKS & SPELLCASTING

NAME	ATK BONUS	DAMAGE\TYPE

FEATURES & TRAITS

PROFICIENCIES & LANGUAGES

EQUIPMENT

CP
SP
EP
GP
PP

49

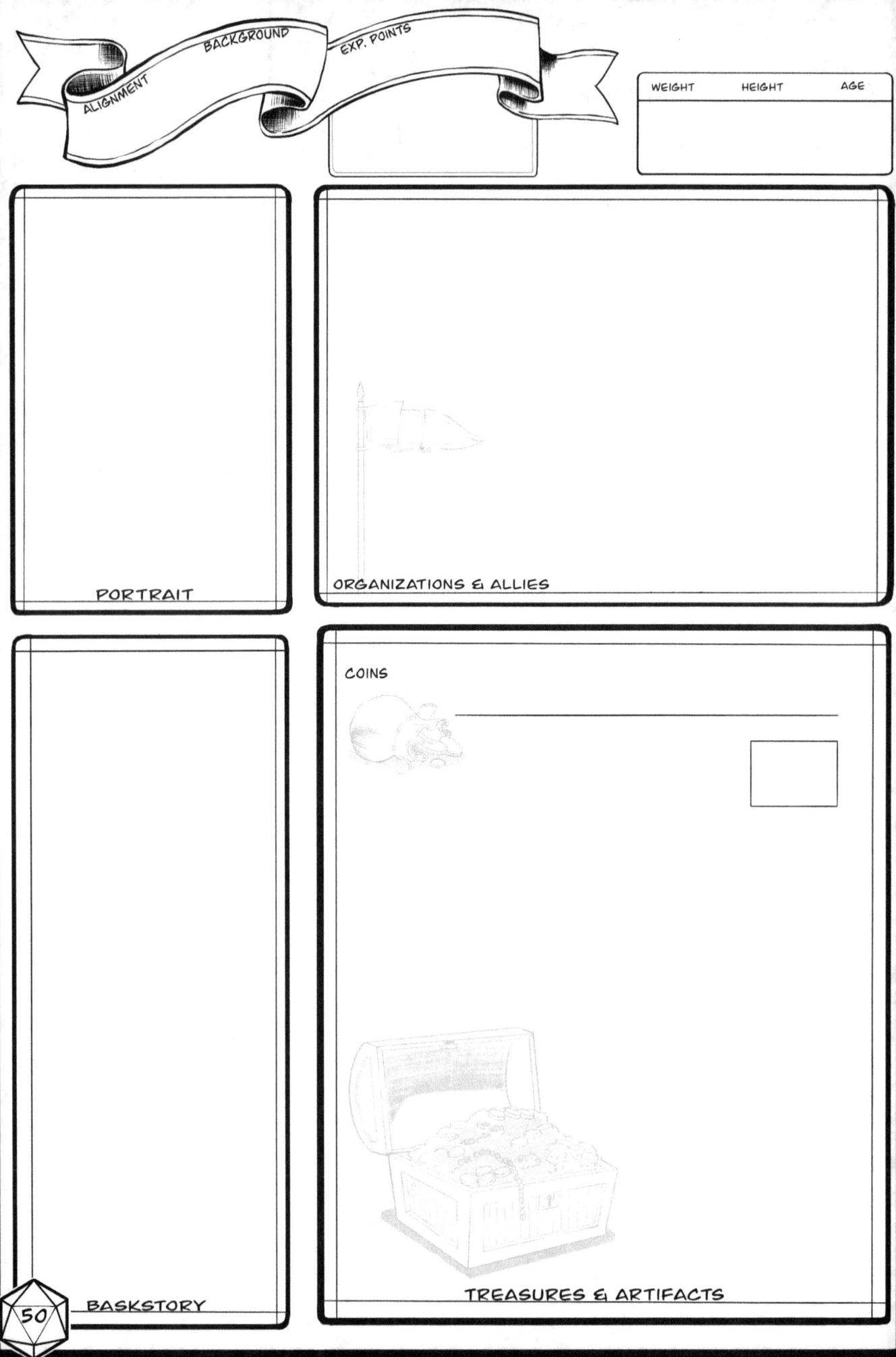

ALIGNMENT   BACKGROUND   EXP. POINTS

WEIGHT   HEIGHT   AGE

PORTRAIT

ORGANIZATIONS & ALLIES

COINS

BASKSTORY

TREASURES & ARTIFACTS

50

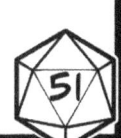

ON THIS PAGE, YOU CAN WRITE DOWN ANY RELEVANT MATTER OF THE STORY AND ADVENTURES THAT YOUR CHARACTER LIVES: THE CLUE ABOUT A TREASURE, THE MAP OF A DUNGEON, RUMORS ABOUT THE WHEREABOUTS OF A RELEVANT PERSON... IT'S YOUR ADVENTURE, MAKE IT EPIC!

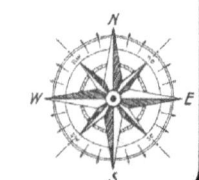

NAME

CLASS   RACE   LvL

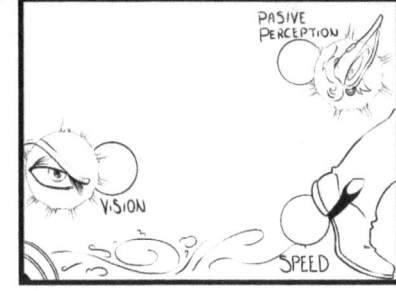

PASIVE PERCEPTION

VISION

SPEED

AC   HP   TEMP HP

HIT DICE

TOTAL _____

SAVING THROWS
- O STRENGHT
- O DEXTERITY
- O CONSTITUTION
- O INTELLIGENCE
- O WISDOM
- O CHARISMA

DEATH   LIVING

INITIATIVE

INSPIRATION

PROFICIENLY BONUS

WEAPONS

NAME	ATK BONUS	RANGE	DAMAGE	TYPE

SKILLS
- O ACROBATICS
- O ANIMAL HANDLING
- O ARCANA
- O ATHLETICS
- O DECEPTION
- O HISTORY
- O INSIGHT
- O INTIMIDATION
- O INVESTIGATION
- O MEDICINE
- O NATURE
- O PERCEPTION
- O PERFORMANCE
- O PERSUASION
- O RELIGION
- O SLEIGHT OF HAND
- O STEALTH
- O SURVIVAL

STRENGTH

DEXTERITY

CONSTITUTION

INTELLIGENCE

WISDOM

CHARISMA

ATTACKS & SPELLCASTING

NAME	ATK BONUS	DAMAGE\TYPE

FEATURES & TRAITS

PROFICIENCIES & LANGUAGES	EQUIPMENT

CP
SP
EP
GP
PP

ALIGNMENT   BACKGROUND   EXP. POINTS

WEIGHT   HEIGHT   AGE

PORTRAIT

ORGANIZATIONS & ALLIES

COINS

BASKSTORY

TREASURES & ARTIFACTS

ON THIS PAGE, YOU CAN WRITE DOWN ANY RELEVANT MATTER OF THE STORY AND ADVENTURES THAT YOUR CHARACTER LIVES: THE CLUE ABOUT A TREASURE, THE MAP OF A DUNGEON, RUMORS ABOUT THE WHEREABOUTS OF A RELEVANT PERSON... IT'S YOUR ADVENTURE, MAKE IT EPIC!

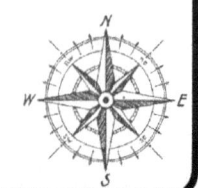

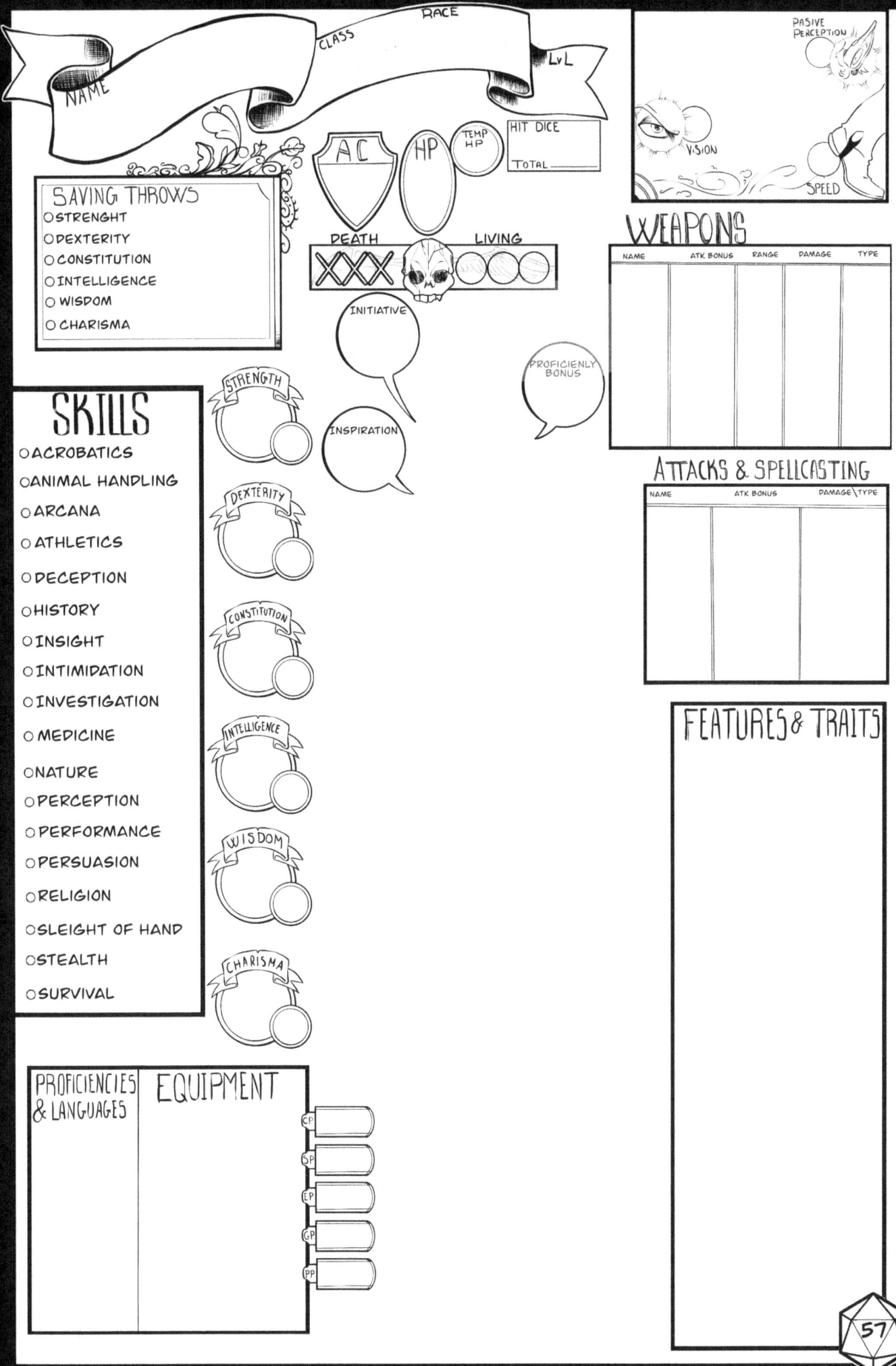

NAME

CLASS RACE LvL

PASSIVE PERCEPTION

VISION SPEED

AC HP TEMP HP

HIT DICE
TOTAL _____

SAVING THROWS
- O STRENGHT
- O DEXTERITY
- O CONSTITUTION
- O INTELLIGENCE
- O WISDOM
- O CHARISMA

DEATH LIVING

INITIATIVE

INSPIRATION

PROFICIENLY BONUS

WEAPONS

NAME	ATK BONUS	RANGE	DAMAGE	TYPE

ATTACKS & SPELLCASTING

NAME	ATK BONUS	DAMAGE\TYPE

SKILLS
- O ACROBATICS
- O ANIMAL HANDLING
- O ARCANA
- O ATHLETICS
- O DECEPTION
- O HISTORY
- O INSIGHT
- O INTIMIDATION
- O INVESTIGATION
- O MEDICINE
- O NATURE
- O PERCEPTION
- O PERFORMANCE
- O PERSUASION
- O RELIGION
- O SLEIGHT OF HAND
- O STEALTH
- O SURVIVAL

STRENGTH

DEXTERITY

CONSTITUTION

INTELLIGENCE

WISDOM

CHARISMA

FEATURES & TRAITS

PROFICIENCIES & LANGUAGES

EQUIPMENT

CP
SP
EP
GP
PP

57

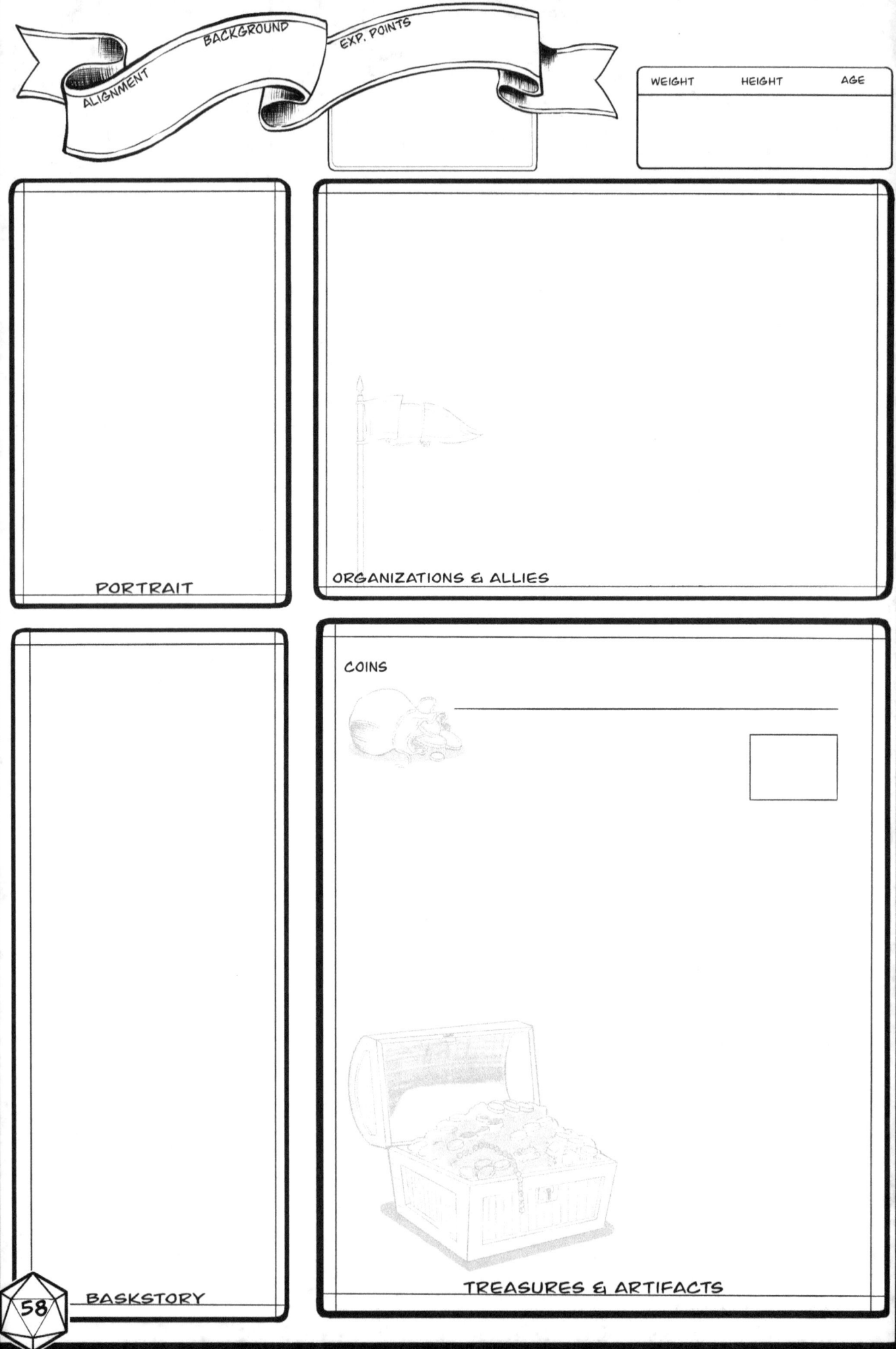

ALIGNMENT   BACKGROUND   EXP. POINTS

WEIGHT   HEIGHT   AGE

PORTRAIT

ORGANIZATIONS & ALLIES

COINS

BASKSTORY

TREASURES & ARTIFACTS

58

ON THIS PAGE, YOU CAN WRITE DOWN ANY RELEVANT MATTER OF THE STORY AND ADVENTURES THAT YOUR CHARACTER LIVES: THE CLUE ABOUT A TREASURE, THE MAP OF A DUNGEON, RUMORS ABOUT THE WHEREABOUTS OF A RELEVANT PERSON... IT'S YOUR ADVENTURE, MAKE IT EPIC!

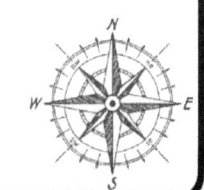

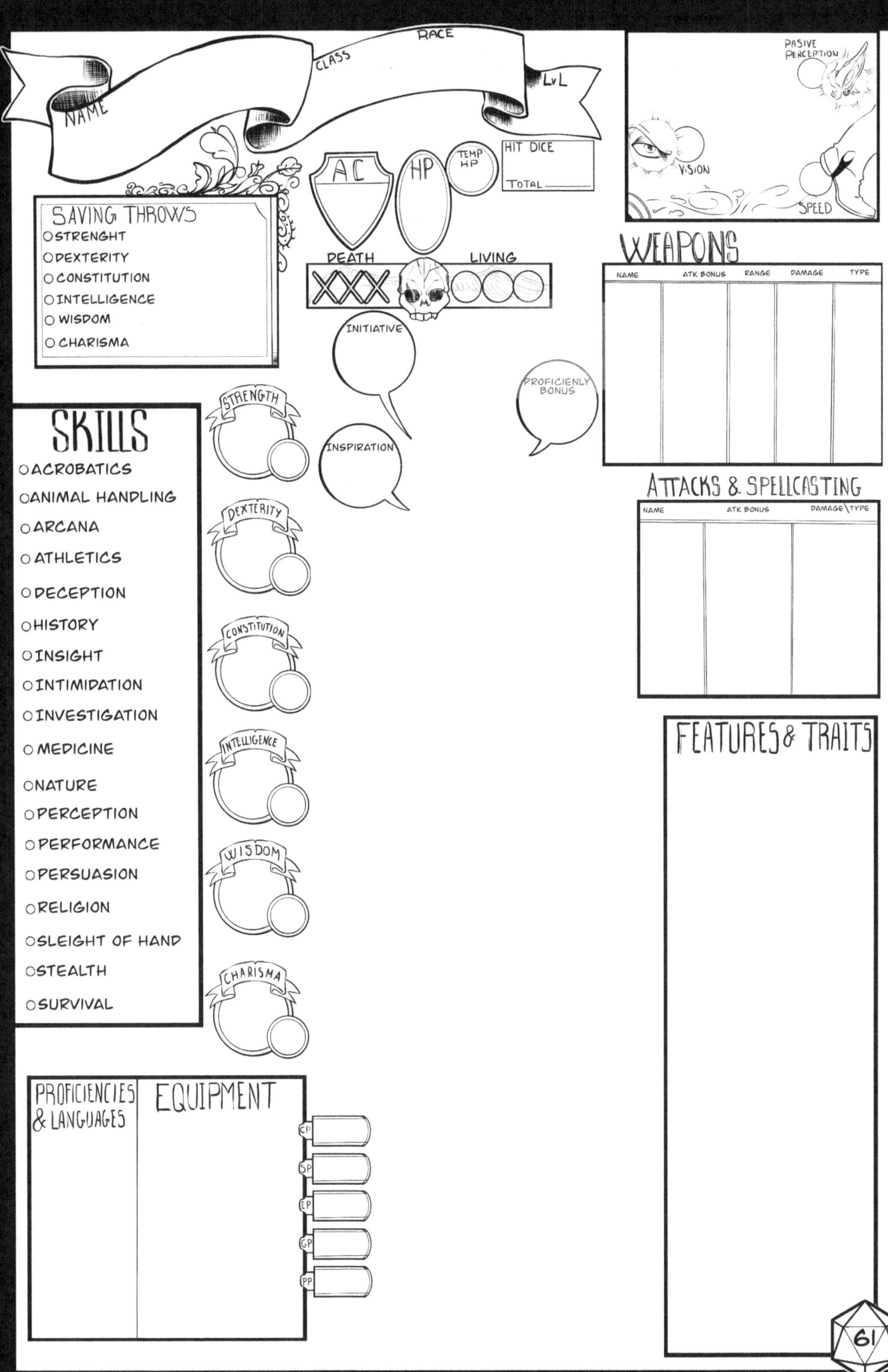

NAME

CLASS　RACE　LvL

PASIVE PERCEPTION

AC

HP

TEMP HP

HIT DICE

TOTAL ____

VISION

SPEED

SAVING THROWS
- STRENGHT
- DEXTERITY
- CONSTITUTION
- INTELLIGENCE
- WISDOM
- CHARISMA

DEATH　　LIVING

INITIATIVE

INSPIRATION

PROFICIENLY BONUS

WEAPONS

NAME	ATK BONUS	RANGE	DAMAGE	TYPE

ATTACKS & SPELLCASTING

NAME	ATK BONUS	DAMAGE\TYPE

SKILLS
- ACROBATICS
- ANIMAL HANDLING
- ARCANA
- ATHLETICS
- DECEPTION
- HISTORY
- INSIGHT
- INTIMIDATION
- INVESTIGATION
- MEDICINE
- NATURE
- PERCEPTION
- PERFORMANCE
- PERSUASION
- RELIGION
- SLEIGHT OF HAND
- STEALTH
- SURVIVAL

STRENGTH

DEXTERITY

CONSTITUTION

INTELLIGENCE

WISDOM

CHARISMA

FEATURES & TRAITS

PROFICIENCIES & LANGUAGES

EQUIPMENT

CP

SP

EP

GP

PP

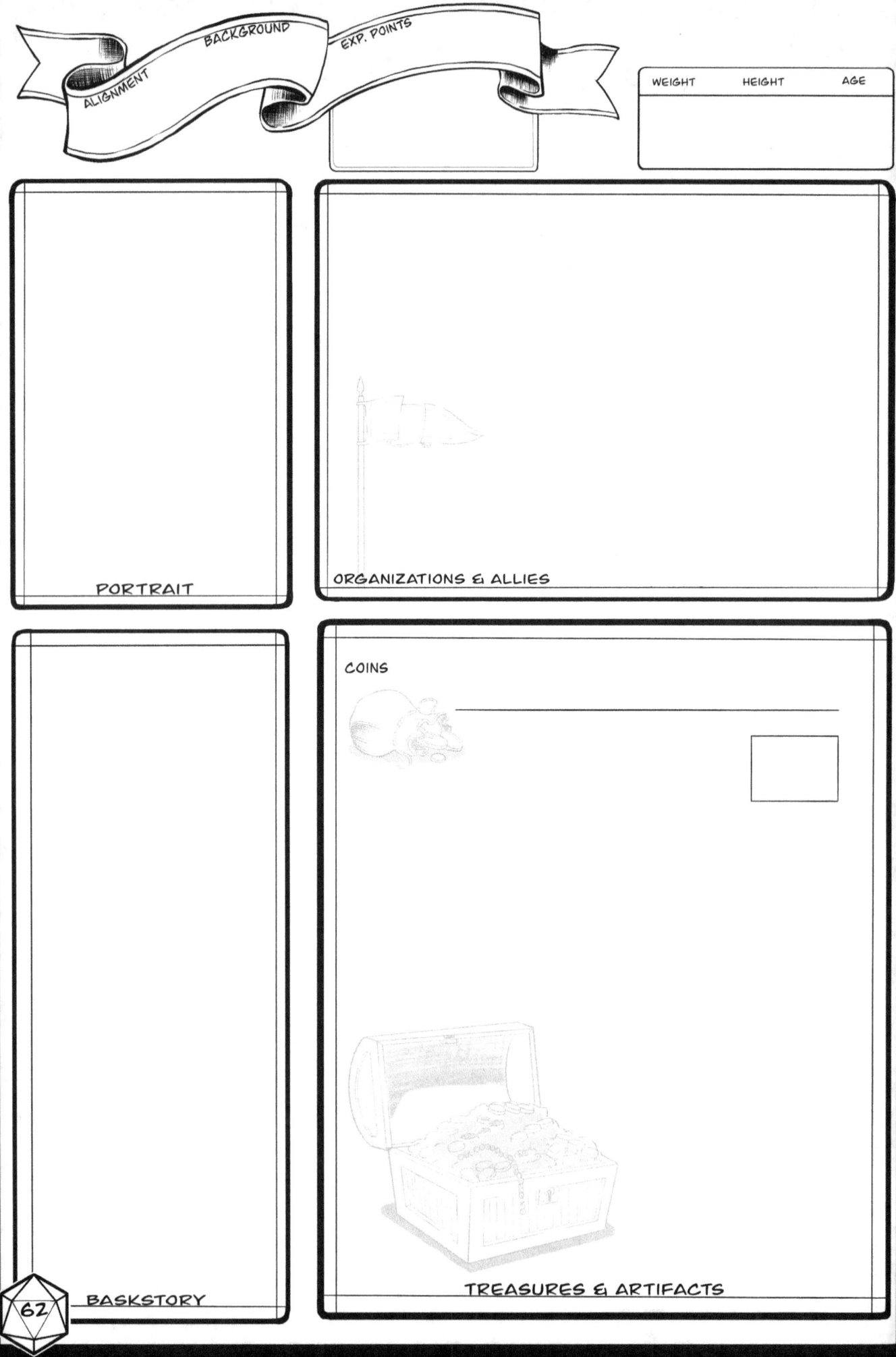

ALIGNMENT   BACKGROUND   EXP. POINTS

WEIGHT   HEIGHT   AGE

PORTRAIT

ORGANIZATIONS & ALLIES

COINS

BASKSTORY

TREASURES & ARTIFACTS

ON THIS PAGE, YOU CAN WRITE DOWN ANY RELEVANT MATTER OF THE STORY AND ADVENTURES THAT YOUR CHARACTER LIVES: THE CLUE ABOUT A TREASURE, THE MAP OF A DUNGEON, RUMORS ABOUT THE WHEREABOUTS OF A RELEVANT PERSON... IT'S YOUR ADVENTURE, MAKE IT EPIC!

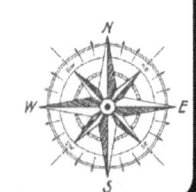

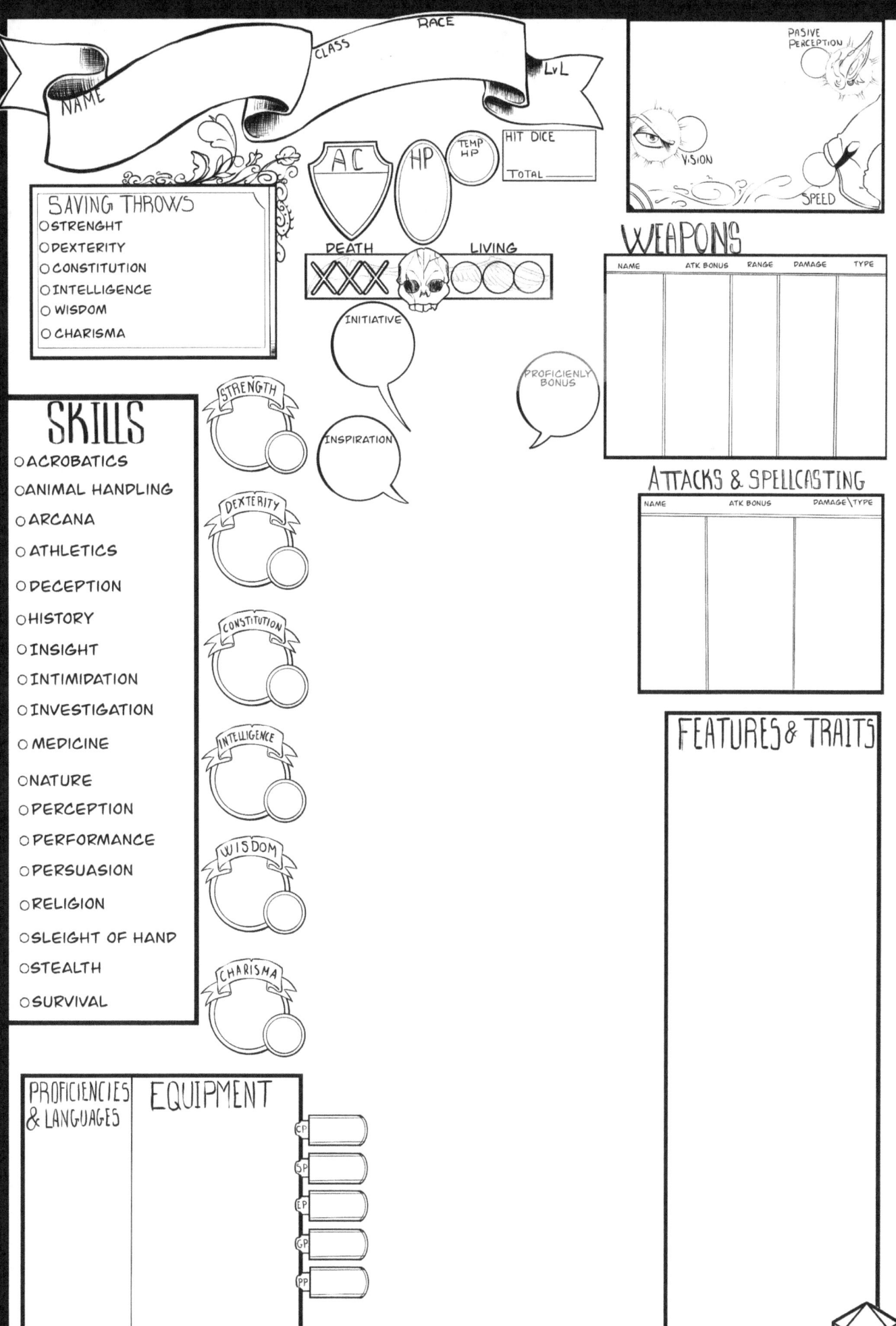

NAME

CLASS RACE LvL

AC HP TEMP HP

HIT DICE
TOTAL _____

PASIVE PERCEPTION

VISION

SPEED

SAVING THROWS
O STRENGHT
O DEXTERITY
O CONSTITUTION
O INTELLIGENCE
O WISDOM
O CHARISMA

DEATH XXX LIVING

INITIATIVE

INSPIRATION

WEAPONS

NAME	ATK BONUS	RANGE	DAMAGE	TYPE

PROFICIENLY BONUS

ATTACKS & SPELLCASTING

NAME	ATK BONUS	DAMAGE\TYPE

SKILLS
O ACROBATICS
O ANIMAL HANDLING
O ARCANA
O ATHLETICS
O DECEPTION
O HISTORY
O INSIGHT
O INTIMIDATION
O INVESTIGATION
O MEDICINE
O NATURE
O PERCEPTION
O PERFORMANCE
O PERSUASION
O RELIGION
O SLEIGHT OF HAND
O STEALTH
O SURVIVAL

STRENGTH

DEXTERITY

CONSTITUTION

INTELLIGENCE

WISDOM

CHARISMA

FEATURES & TRAITS

PROFICIENCIES & LANGUAGES

EQUIPMENT

CP
SP
EP
GP
PP

65

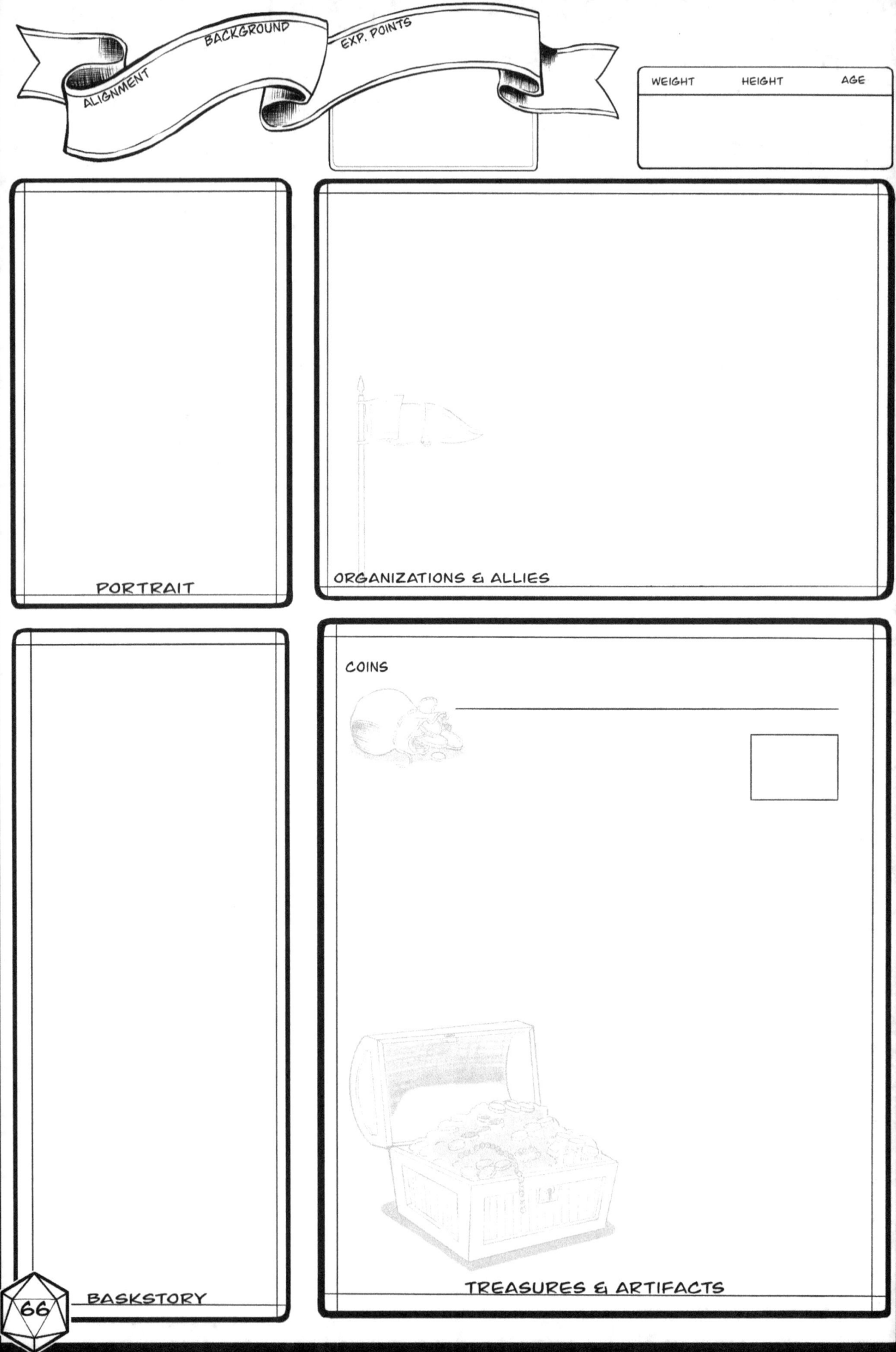

ALIGNMENT BACKGROUND EXP. POINTS

WEIGHT   HEIGHT   AGE

PORTRAIT

ORGANIZATIONS & ALLIES

COINS

BASKSTORY

TREASURES & ARTIFACTS

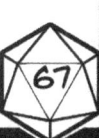

ON THIS PAGE, YOU CAN WRITE DOWN ANY RELEVANT MATTER OF THE STORY AND ADVENTURES THAT YOUR CHARACTER LIVES: THE CLUE ABOUT A TREASURE, THE MAP OF A DUNGEON, RUMORS ABOUT THE WHEREABOUTS OF A RELEVANT PERSON... IT'S YOUR ADVENTURE, MAKE IT EPIC!

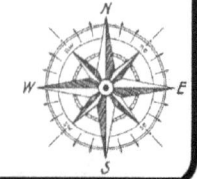

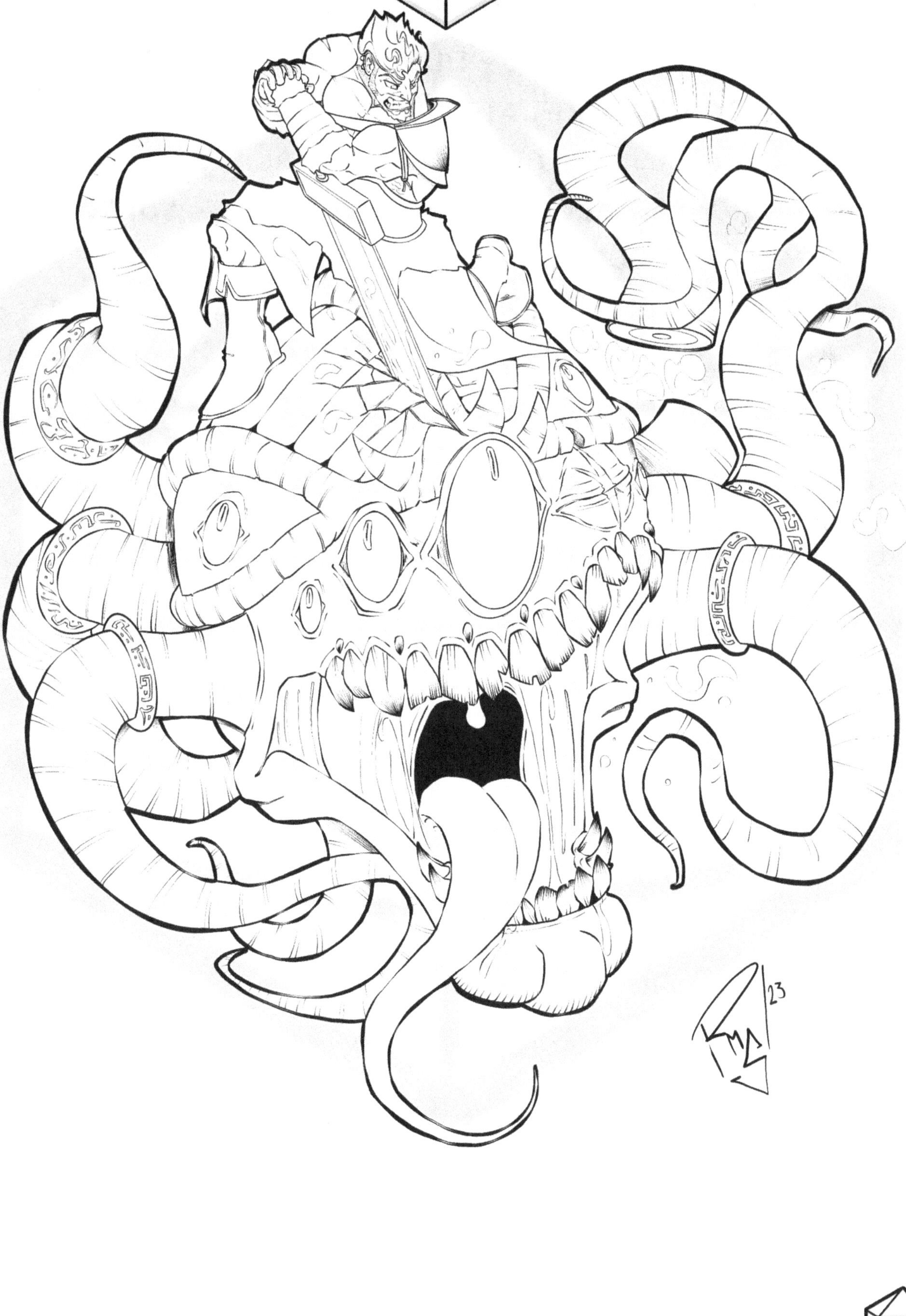

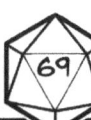

THANK YOU FOR PURCHASING MY FIRST BOOK. I HOPE YOU ENJOYED MY ART. WITH YOUR SUPPORT YOU HELP ME TO KEEP CREATING CONTENT, AND SOON I WILL CONTINUE PUBLISHING MORE BOOKS AND CONTENT RELATED TO FANTASY AND THE ROLEPLAYING WORLD IN GENERAL, AS I AM PASSIONATE ABOUT DOING IT, AND THE WORLD NEEDS PEOPLE WHO LOVE WHAT THEY DO. FOLLOW ME ON INSTAGRAM, @RICKYCARTOONART , AS I'LL START DOING GIVEAWAYS AND CONTESTS THERE, AND YOU'LL BE ABLE TO KEEP UP WITH MY NEXT CREATIONS. BEST REGARDS!!!

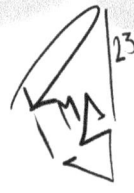

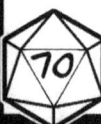

www.ingramcontent.com/pod-product-compliance
Lightning Source LLC
Chambersburg PA
CBHW082226290526
45794CB00009B/3691